THE PALMER METHOD OF
BUSINESS WRITING

*A Series of Self-teaching Lessons in Rapid,
Plain, Unshaded, Coarse-pen, Muscular
Movement Writing for Use in All Schools,
Public or Private, Where an Easy and
Legible Handwriting is the Object Sought*

BY

A. N. PALMER

British Library Cataloguing-in-Publication Data
A catalogue record for this book is available from the
British Library

CONTENTS

Austin Norman Palmer

Austin Norman Palmer was born on 22 December 1860 in Fort Jackson, St. Lawrence County, New York, USA. He is best known as an innovator in the field of penmanship and the creator of the *Palmer Method* of script.

Palmer spent his early youth on the family farm in Fort Jackson, until the death of his father in 1873. The family then moved to Manchester, New Hampshire.

After completing public school, Palmer's mother encouraged him to enter the business college of the famed penman George Gaskell, and it was here that Palmer became inspired by the variety and beauty of the craft. He attained substantial proficiency in ornamental writing, and upon his graduation, was awarded a letter of recommendation from Gaskell himself.

Palmer went on to teach courses in penmanship in Rockville, Indiana, and St. Joseph, Missouri. In 1800, Palmer was given the chance to practically apply his skills in penmanship, and was offered a position with the *Iowa Railroad Land Company*. Whilst this job did not allow him full remit to demonstrate skills such as flourished birds and shaded capitals, Palmer did notice that it was customary for all ornamental penmen to flourish capitals with a free arm swing, with the arm completely off the desk – whilst the clerks were able to achieve greater speed and accuracy through smaller movements of the fingers and wrist. This discovery, of what he called 'muscular movement' prompted Palmer to reconceptualise the art of penmanship. To this end, he started producing a magazine, *The Western Penman,* first published in 1884, in order to attract a larger audience to his method. For the next sixteen years, Palmer taught his method in various cities in the Mid-West, and in 1888 published *Palmer's Guide to Muscular Movement Writing.* His success teaching large classes of students in business college's convinced Palmer that anyone could learn to write with a free, tireless hand, utilising his new method. He consequently transcribed reports of all his lessons, releasing them as a series in the *Penman,* beginning in 1899. The success of this endeavour greatly increased Palmer's fame, and in 1904 he conducted a penmanship exhibition which generated nation-wide attention. The Palmer method was most notably adopted in the schools of New York City in 1905, after the Associate Superintendent of the City attended the exhibition. In 1915 Palmer's system received the Gold Medal at the *Panama Pacific Exposition* in San Francisco, and in 1926, the Gold Medal at the *Sesqui Centennial Exposition* in Philadelphia.

Palmer remained essentially a teacher for his entire life, never tiring in his energy and enthusiasm for the art of penmanship. He died on 16 November 1927 at the age of sixty-six. By the time of his death, it has been estimated that over 25 million Americans were taught writing from the Palmer Method of penmanship.

AN EXPLANATION

The object of this book is to teach rapid, easily-executed, business writing. It has not been written to exploit any one's skill as a pen artist. It aims to be of use to those who are ambitious to become good, practical business writers. The lessons it contains are not experimental, but have been the means of guiding millions of boys and girls, young men and women to a good business style of writing.

As will be seen at a glance, the Palmer Method of Business Writing has nothing in common with copy-books which have been so largely used in public schools for more than half a century. If they are right, this book is wrong. The two methods of teaching writing are absolutely antagonistic.

In teaching writing, as in other subjects, the final result should be the criterion. Pupils who follow absolutely the Palmer Method plan never fail to become good penmen. On the other hand, no one ever learned to write a good, free, rapid, easy, and legible hand from any copy-book that was ever made.

The copy-book has but one purpose—to secure absolute mechanical accuracy. The copy-book headline is usually first carefully penciled by a skilled penman after a given model, and shows none of the individuality of the penman employed in its construction. The penciled copy is given to a skilled script-engraver, who engraves it by hand and further perfects it wherever possible. This impossible and lifeless ideal the child is required to imitate through long, dreary pages of copying. No wonder he fails!

It has been proved, through at least two generations, that the copy-book kills individuality and makes freedom of movement impossible. It compels slow finger-action in the formation of letters, giving a fair degree of accuracy where only slow writing is required; but the pupil's work inevitably becomes scribbling when the least speed is attempted. In the Palmer Method, freedom of movement is the foundation, and, through a constantly repeated series of rapid drills, the application of movement becomes a fixed habit of the learner. Under this plan the pupil's first attempt is naturally crude, but every drill practiced in strict accord with the printed instructions tends to add grace and accuracy to his work. The sure result is a handwriting that embodies these four essentials—legibility, rapidity, case, and endurance.

The drills and copies in this book are actual writing, executed with a rapid, easy, muscular movement, and then photo-engraved, thus retaining the individuality of the writer.

Pupils practicing from these lessons acquire the general style of the copies, but, at the same time, there is left to them the possibility of developing their own individuality.

SOME PALMER METHOD FACTS -

A PERSONAL TALK

**Read and Carefully Consider Everything on
These Three Pages Before Beginning the Study
and Practice of the Lessons. Failing to follow
These Simple Suggestions, You are Likely to
Waste Many Hours, Weeks, and Months in
Useless Practice**

THE PALMER METHOD is a text-book on practical writing and should be studied as such—not treated as a copy-book. The printed instructions are the author's direct personal talks to pupils—the same things he would say to you from day to day were he personally to teach you. These instructions are of more importance than the copies. They tell you how to develop and use the muscular movement in writing. If you do not follow the instructions, you will fail.

Pupils who followed absolutely the Palmer Method plan have always learned to write well. Pupils who have not first studied the plainly printed directions and followed them absolutely, have partly or completely failed. Failure is unnecessary.

Thousands of young men and women have made the Palmer

Method of Business Writing the stepping-stone to positions in business offices, where commercial advancement rewarded faithful service.

In hundreds of classes where the Palmer Method has been faithfully studied and completely mastered, periods devoted to written spelling, composition, examinations, and other written work have been reduced more than half. Time thus saved has been put to very good use in other directions. In the beginning stages of the work, until good position, muscular relaxation, correct and comfortable penholding, and muscular movement as a habit in writing have been acquired, extra practice may be necessary; but the extra time will be saved many times over in all written work later.

Muscular movement writing means good, healthful posture, straight spinal columns, eyes far enough away from the paper for safety, and both shoulders of equal height. These features alone should be sufficient to encourage boys and girls to master a physical training system of writing such as is presented in the following pages, remembering that it is impossible to do good muscular movement writing in twisted, unhealthful positions, or with stiff and rigid muscles.

Straight line and oval drills are of no value except as they lead to writing. They are the means through which to gain the muscular control that will enable pupils to master an ideal permanent style of rapid, plain-as-print writing.

When pupils have learned good posture, correct penholding,

and how to use muscular movement in making a good two-space compact oval, they are ready to begin to learn how to write well. Too many pupils think they have really learned how to write well when they are able to make some of the very simple drills in correct posture at the right speed and in correct rhythm. That is really the starting-point toward good penmanship, and should be followed immediately by the practice of words, and, indeed, by the use of the movement in all written work.

Study and practice go hand in hand in securing the best results in the shortest possible time. Keep the Manual open before you as you practice; study and make frequent and careful comparisons of your work with the drills if you wish to make rapid progress.

Your letters, words, and sentences should occupy the same amount of space they do in the Manual. Always, before beginning practice, the drill should be studied in every little detail until the correct picture is in your mind.

Just how and where does the first line in a letter begin; is it made with an upward or downward stroke; how high is the letter; how wide is each part; how much running space does it occupy; in what direction should the pen move in beginning, continuing, and completing the letter; and at what rate of speed should the letter or word be written? These are questions that should constantly occupy you as soon as automatic muscular movement has been established. In fact, as was said before, study and practice must go hand in hand, if good results are to be the outcome.

Blackboard copies, though written by expert penmen, are seen at many different angles, and at different distances, and do not give correct mental impressions.

It is highly important not only that pupils have copies of the Manual, but that they study the printed instructions and drills, closely and constantly.

The plainly printed instructions in the Palmer Method tell you step by step exactly what to do and how to do it, in order to progress steadily and surely toward the desired end.

Millions of American boys and girls have learned a permanent style of rapid, easy, legible, and beautiful writing by carefully and patiently following the printed directions found in the Palmer Method of Business Writing. Final results have then been delightful to pupils, teachers, parents, and school officials.

The first step is a correct understanding of the required position. Study the pictures on pages twelve, fourteen, and fifteen, of a pupil who has learned how to sit so as to use the large tireless muscles of his arms to the best possible advantage. Study every little detail of these pictures from the crown of the head to the shoes. Study particularly and closely the arms, the relation of one arm to the other, the position at the desk, the distance of the body from the desk, and the positions of the fingers preparatory to taking the penholder.

As progress is made in the more advanced lessons, you should refer frequently to these pictures and try to sit as this pupil sat when his photographs were taken for the Palmer Method. When writing, he always sits as shown in these photographs, and he knows that it would be physically impossible to use muscular movement writing in a cramped, unhealthful position.

There is an old saying, "Practice makes perfect." That is only partly true in relation to writing. Practice of the right kind leads toward perfection, but the wrong kind of practice leads just as surely in the opposite direction. It is not so much the exercise that is practiced as the manner in which it is practiced. Millions of pupils have wasted the time given to movement exercises because they thought it was the exercise that counted and not the manner in which it was made.

There is no value in any penmanship drill ever invented unless it is practiced with correct positions of body, arms, fingers, penholders, paper, and with exactly the right movement, and at exactly the right rate of speed.

If you study the instructions in the Palmer Method, and follow them absolutely in daily practice, you will make steady progress and, within a short time, become a splendid penman. But, even should you spend a great deal of time practicing the drills in a poor position with cramped muscles and with the wrong movement, you not only will make no progress toward good writing, but will contract bad habits, or firmly fix those already established, and, under such conditions, the possibility of learning to write well will constantly become more and more remote.

It is a fact, that among the thousands of men and women employed in business offices who do longhand writing constantly, rapidly, and well, none can be found who do not use muscular movement, because it is the only movement through which penmanship embracing in the highest degree legibility, rapidity, ease, and endurance can be developed.

It is now generally conceded that systems of copy-books have inevitably resulted in a poor finished product of penmanship. Public school officials and teachers were satisfied with copy-books so long as they did not consider good posture, muscular relaxation, easy, tireless movement and reasonable speed, as important factors. Then the discovery was made that pupils were able to draw the letters slowly and very accurately in close imitation of mechanically engraved copies, but that when rapid, continuous writing was required in the penmanship employed in written spelling, compositions, examinations, etc., the letter forms became dissipated in appearance and soon approached the stage of scribbling.

It must be conceded by everyone that any system of writing which does not lead to an automatic style embodying legibility, rapidity, ease, and endurance is a failure.

The term "Copy-book" has been applied for many years to sheets of paper bound together with a cover, containing at the top of each page, a line of writing or an exercise to be imitated by the pupils on the lines below. Sometimes the headlines are made from carefully penciled copies, mechanically perfected through a system of hand engraving.

There are also bound books, with copies at the top of the pages that were really written with some show of muscular movement and afterward photo-engraved, but the copy-book principles are involved in the publication of such books— principles which preclude the teaching of good writing through their use. The mental attitude of pupils who see before them the immaculate page upon which they must make reproductions, as nearly facsimile as possible of the copies at the top, is wholly unfavorable to the process.

Another recent copy-book system is the pad with the copy at the top, and sometimes at the top and center of each page, there being blank lines below for practice purposes. These modified copy-books are probably doing just as much harm to the cause of practical writing as the former kind. Unless the mental attitude is right, physical conditions will be wrong.

Sincerely,

A. N. Palmer

FIRST SPECIMENS

Beginning pupils should write three sets of first specimens on paper about 8×10½ inches. One set should be kept by the teacher, another retained by the pupil, and one set sent to the nearest office of The A. N. Palmer Company.

The value of these first specimens will be clearly apparent as the work of muscular movement development and application progresses and comparisons are made. Those sent to the publication office are alphabetically arranged and kept for future reference. When pupils have mastered the movement and become good business writers, their second specimens should be sent to be filed with the first. The improvement is often so great that the first and second specimens may be engraved and published with great credit to the schools, the pupils, and the Palmer Method.

In these specimens the following form should be followed: On the first line write the name, the age, and the grade; on the second line, the name of the school, city or town, and the date. Skip one line and make a set of capitals; skip a line and make two lines of miscellaneous figures; skip a line and write, "A specimen of my best writing before I began to practice muscular movement writing from the lessons in the Palmer Method of Business Writing." The above was written in. . . . . minutes and. . . . . seconds.

CLOTHING FOR THE RIGHT FOREARM

As the muscles of the right forearm play an important part in the movement, it is necessary that they should be so clothed as to permit, at all times, unrestricted action. Many good writers consider this of such importance that they cut off the right undersleeve at the elbow. **To the Teacher**: See that pupils' arms are free of heavy clothing.

WRITING MATERIALS

Not much progress can be made with poor paper, poor pens, or poor ink. Good materials are a necessity. Do not use a penholder covered with metal where the fingers rest if another can be procured. Never use an oblique penholder in business writing. It is out of place and of no advantage whatever. Nothing equals an oblique holder for ornamental writing, but there its utility ends. Use paper of generous size for your practice, a medium coarse pen, and ink that flows well. Blue-black writing fluid is the best.

Study the instructions; they are of more importance than the copies.

LESSON 1

CORRECT POSITIONS FOR CLASS ROOM WRITING

IN the following pages are reproduced photographs of a class of students who are experts in the Palmer Method writing. While they knew that their photographs were to be taken, they did not change their every-day penmanship positions in the least particular. It was not necessary, because they had all acquired the habit of sitting in positions that are comfortable and which at the same time permit muscular freedom and control.

In elementary schools in cities, space is so limited that the use of tables or desks large enough to permit the square front position for writing is usually impossible. If the desks are too small for the square front position the half-right side position may be used.

Study these pictures closely; it will pay.

In the first picture, notice that the right elbow rests on or near the lower right corner of the desk. This position may be occasionally modified to suit the needs of pupils. As an example, a very fat boy or girl may find it necessary to let the right arm rest over on the desk a little farther.

A good rule to follow in finding the correct position of the right arm on the desk for writing is as follows: Place the body at the desk in the correct square front position, raise the entire right arm a few inches, and withdrawing control, let it drop. Wherever it strikes the desk it should remain. To draw the arm toward the side would force the right shoulder upward into an uncomfortable, unhealthful position, or would force the pupil to lean backward. On the other hand, to place the right arm farther over on the desk would force the body too far forward.

These photographs show that the pupils sit comfortably in the seats; that the upper ends of their penholders point a little to the right of their right shoulders—usually half way between the elbow and the shoulder; that the Palmer Method is placed at the upper left corner of the desk—being held open at the required drill with a rubber band; that the left forearm is on the desk in such a position as will keep the body upright, the left shoulder from drooping, reserving the free use of the left hand for changing the positions of the Manual and the paper as required.

In this position it is easy to push the sheet of paper forward as progress is made toward the bottom of the page; also to move the paper to the left when the writing has reached a third or half the distance across a line, and back into the first position for a new line.

The exact position of the body at the desk and the relative positions of the left and right arms in writing are very clearly shown in illustration two, while the position of the left arm in its relation to desk, Manual, and paper, is best shown in illustration three.

No student who fails in the matter of position will master muscular movement writing. Correct position is of the greatest importance, and it should be studied and thoroughly mastered before the writing itself is considered.

To the Teacher: At this point, pupils should be required to close their Methods and show their familiarity with the preceding discussion of position by answering questions relating to it, and also to assume the position described several times, to prove their working knowledge of it.

Position illustration number 1. Read page 7 for instructions.

Position illustration number 2. Read page 7 for instructions.

Position illustration number 3. Read page 7 for instructions.

LESSON 2

PHYSICAL TRAINING IN PENMANSHIP PRACTICE

Correct Posture, Relaxing Exercises, Movement Practice, and Penholding, Taught in Pictures

NO progress can be made in mastering good muscular movement writing until there is a correct understanding of the important steps and the order in which they must be taken.

No written or spoken words can explain these more fully and plainly than the fifteen accompanying pictures given as models. They tell all that could be told about the important

20

beginning steps, and they should be studied with thoroughness now, and often during future practice periods.

Step one, illustration four: Position in seat with arms hanging limply at the sides. **Step two,** number five: Body turned a little to the left and arms extended above the desk, wrists and fingers limp. **Step three,** number six: After permitting both arms to drop to the desk, raise right arm as shown in the picture, withdraw control and let it drop, repeating the operation until the arm drops comfortably into the writing position, with a square turn at the elbow and fingers bent naturally. **Step four,** number seven: **Learn to run the writing machine.**

Notice the closed fingers making a fist, and the absorbed interest with which this boy studies his arm near the elbow. The arm is the machine, and the engine that moves it is above the elbow. With the arm lying on the desk in that position, it requires but little effort to drive the wrist forward out of, and to pull it backward into, the sleeve; this is "muscular movement." Fix in your mind the following facts: In muscular movement writing the arm is never raised above, but lies on the desk all the time in a perfectly natural, comfortable position; the sleeve remains in one place on the desk at all times, and the flesh on the arm moves, the action being inside the sleeve.

Careful study of illustrations nine and ten at this point will be helpful. The arrow points to the main rest, which should always be the larger part of the forearm near the elbow. In writing, the wrist and side of the hand should never touch the paper. There are only two rests, the muscle near the elbow, as explained, and the third and fourth fingers, those fingers supplying a movable rest, and gliding over the paper in the various directions in which the pen moves.

Do not think of writing or penholding at this point, but give all your attention to position, muscular relaxation, and the running of the writing machine, until good position and easy movement have become natural. It often pays primary grade pupils to practice on position, relaxing exercises, and movement, from three to six weeks before taking writing instruments. It is best that all beginners on muscular movement practice should devote several periods to these things before thinking of penholding or writing.

Future progress depends upon present understanding of these first important steps. Even after beginning the movement drills, and when muscular movement is used in all writing, parts of practice periods should be devoted to the study of the writing machine, and to the calisthenic exercises suggested.

Illustration number eight is worthy of close study and imitation. This boy was looking at some object at a distance. In this position you should practice the movement. Test the movement here, and see if you can feel the action of the muscle of the forearm as it rests on the desk.

No. 4   No. 5   No. 6   No. 7   No. 8

DEFINITION OF MOVEMENT

Muscular movement as applied to writing, is the movement of the muscles of the arm from the shoulder to the wrist, with the larger part of the arm below the elbow on the desk, the fingers not being held rigid, but remaining passive, and neither extended nor contracted in the formation of letters. In this movement the driving power is located above the elbow in the upper muscles of the arm.

Examine your right arm. Notice the increasing size from the wrist to the elbow. Note particularly the elasticity of the muscles. On the elasticity and development of those muscles depends your success in learning a good style of writing. (Reread this and make sure that you thoroughly understand what muscular movement means before going ahead, because your success depends upon it.)

HOW TO DEVELOP MUSCULAR ACTION

Place your arm on the desk and close the fingers of the right hand tightly. (Number nine.) See how far you can move the hand forward and backward without slipping the sleeve or without any motion of the wrist or fingers.

Can you move that hand through space a sufficient distance to make any capital? Could you make a capital through two or three lines of the paper, two or three times larger than necessary, without any action of the fingers?

To the Teacher: You should again examine your students on lesson one and also on this lesson.

No. 9   No. 10

ON page fourteen are five pictures of a boy who sits in a splendid position for writing. He is never found in a cramped or poor position. In number eleven, the right elbow is placed on the lower right corner, the hand pointed toward the upper left corner, of the desk. The arm may then be lowered until it rests in a writing position. In number twelve, the left arm is placed on the desk as shown in pictures one, two, and three, and then the exercise of the muscles begins. The entire right arm is on the desk, and this is the best position, except when the arm is so thin that the bone of the elbow grates on the

24

desk. Then the elbow may be extended off the desk enough to relieve the discomfort.

In no case will it be necessary to extend the elbow more than an inch; and not one pupil in a hundred will need to take advantage of this exception to the rule, that the entire right arm should be on the desk.

In number thirteen, make a special study of the upper part of the penholder. It does not point toward the right shoulder, and never will, if the arm, wrist, and hand are allowed to retain natural positions, providing pupil and desk are fitted to each other. In number fourteen, again study the right arm, and, in particular, notice its distance from the right side, also look at the portion of the penholder in sight.

In number fifteen, notice carefully the distance between the boy and the desk. You should always sit well back in your seat, so far back that the body will not touch the desk. This boy is none too far back; his writing is well in front of the eyes, and it is easy for him to retain the very important square turn at the right elbow. You should follow his good example in the matter of position, and if you practice faithfully you can soon become an expert penman.

Number sixteen shows the position in which many good business penmen carry the penholder when writing. Others who write just as well let the holder drop below the knuckle joint, as shown in illustrations twenty-four and twenty-five, page seventeen. The best position is determined by the length of the fingers and the shape of the hand. It is not necessary that the pupil with a long, slim hand and long, tapering fingers, should carry his penholder in exactly the same position as the pupil with the short, thick hand and short, stubby fingers.

No. 11   No. 12   No. 13   No. 14   No. 15

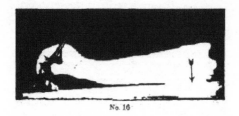

No. 16

No. 17   No. 18   No. 19   No. 20   No. 21

LESSON 3

Here are additional pictures from which you are expected

to learn more about the best position for muscular movement writing. See the right (square) turn of his right arm at the elbow; the position in the seat; the position of the back; the distance between the boy and the desk; the positions of the left arm and the left hand; and the distance between the eyes and the paper.

In this lesson you should review all that was said in lessons one and two about important beginning steps, position, muscular relaxation, and penholding. Practice movement (running the writing machine) a few minutes without the penholder, then slip the penholder into the right hand from the left, and practice the movement without touching the pen to the paper, still watching the arm closely, and giving more attention to correct position and movement than to anything else.

Are you comfortable in your seat; do your arms feel comfortable; and are you holding the penholder lightly in the hand without pinching it? Give close attention to these things.

In the next lesson more particular attention will be given to penholding.

TIME REQUIRED TO LEARN

The process of learning a good style of muscular movement writing may be made easy or difficult, short or long, possible or impossible, according to the mental attitudes of teacher and pupil, and the exactness with which directions in this Manual are followed.

Pupils who constantly practice the movement drills in poor positions with incorrect movement never even get started, and pupils who practice from fifteen to thirty minutes a day in good positions with correct movement, but who fall back into the old bad cramped positions and finger movement habits in all other writing, do not get beyond the beginning stages, no matter how many years they may practice.

The pupil who becomes the absolute master of a finished style of muscular movement writing within the limits of six months or one school year is he who gives the closest attention to every detail relating to the beginning steps, who follows the printed instructions closely, who sits in correct position at all times, and uses muscular movement throughout the writing lessons, and in all his written work within a month from the time he begins to study the Palmer Method.

Without conflicting with other subjects it is possible to lay the foundation for an excellent handwriting in one school year, with but fifteen to thirty minutes daily study and practice, and the employment of muscular movement in all written work just as soon as possible. As progress is made in the grades the use of muscular movement can be permanently established.

The boy becomes an expert ball-player by playing ball. At first he is awkward and uncertain, but, as he studies the methods of those who have become experts, and continues to practice, he takes on self-confidence, and finally develops into an expert, even though he could not hit a single ball during his first few games. Boys and girls who learn to skate with almost consummate grace must pass through the awkward stages, when they sit down instead of standing up as they had planned, and when their feet take possession and run away with them. In instrumental music of any kind one does not become an expert without first learning how to practice and then practicing in exactly the right way according to methods prescribed by master teachers. It is the same in penmanship: first, learn how to practice and then practice faithfully. Acquire elasticity, lightness, and freedom, and do not mind if the pen runs away at first and makes some awkward letters. This is to be expected. But stick to the right plan, and gradually you will gain control of the writing muscles of the arm, and with close attention to general form, size, slant, spacing, and correct movement application, you will become a splendid muscular movement penman in a few short months.

HAND, FINGER, AND PENHOLDER STUDIES

STUDY closely the illustrations on this page. In number 22, the fingers bend naturally as in repose, and their positions should remain the same when the penholder is in the hand.

In numbers twenty-four and twenty-five, you should study the relation of the penholder to the hand. As you see, it is a little below the knuckle joint. The first finger bends naturally, and rests on top of the holder about one inch from the point of the pen; the thumb rests on the holder nearly opposite the first joint of the first finger, and the third and fourth fingers are bent, touching the paper and forming a movable rest. Whether these fingers bend exactly as the illustrations show will depend upon their shape and length. It does not matter whether they rest on the nails or sides, if they are comfortable and can be used easily as the movable rest.

22

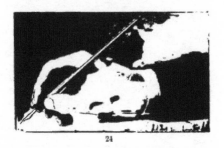

24

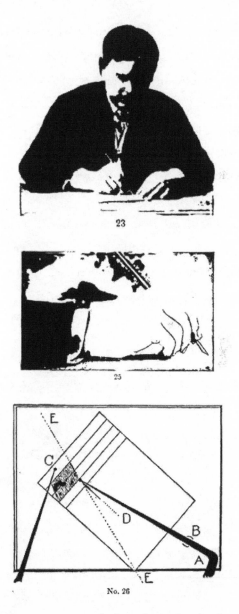

THESE diagrams are intended to show clearly the position of

the writing paper on the desk, the relative positions of arms, paper and desk, and the direction in which the pen moves to secure uniform slant. Number twenty-six is the half-side position mostly used in public schools and best adapted to them, because of the character of the desks. Number twenty-seven is the square front position.

In both diagrams, A represents the square turn at the right elbow and its position on the desk, B is the muscular rest of the forearm, C the position of the left hand in its relation to the paper and the right hand, D the penholder, and E E the imaginary line between the eyes along which the pen should travel in upward and downward strokes.

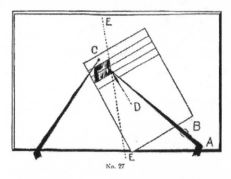

No. 27

With the right forearm crossing the lower edge of the paper a little to the right of the center, the pen should progress one-fourth or one-third of the distance across a sheet of paper eight inches wide, before the position of the paper is changed. Always use the left hand to move the paper. Paper 8×10½ inches in width should be moved three or four times in the progress of the pen across it. When the end of the line has been reached, the paper should be returned to its original position, and should be moved up on the desk the width of one line. Lift the pen before moving the paper.

It is not Palmer Method if the lines are tremulous. Study instructions for speed requirements

LESSON 4

Now the serious work of using and applying the correct movement begins. Before attempting to make any part of drill one, review lessons one, two, and three, and give the closest possible attention to position, muscular relaxation, and penholding. Don't practice before you know how. With the left hand, move the paper to the left three times at equal intervals, in the progress of the pen across it.

Drill 1

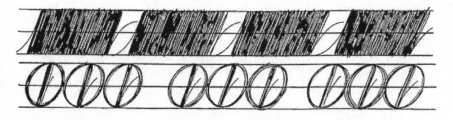

Letting the distance between the two ruled lines, three-eighths of an inch apart, represent one space in height, any part of this drill should be two spaces high. Look at these drills until you have a good mental picture of the height, proportions, and general appearance.

In connection with the straight line part of the drill, study closely diagrams twenty-six and twenty-seven on page eighteen. There is no value in this straight line exercise unless practiced with a forward and backward motion, from and toward the center of the body, with the paper held in the correct position.

If you cannot make the several parts of drill one high enough at first with pure muscular movement, practice without touching the pen to the paper until you have developed more muscular freedom.

In the second line of drill one, the traced oval should first contain six, and later, as a lighter movement is developed, ten revolutions. In this drill it will be well to make first the straight line on the correct slant, and then the oval enclosing it. This order may be changed frequently and the ovals made first. This is an important drill as it has a very specific bearing upon slant.

To the Teacher: It may be profitable for third, fourth, and fifth year pupils to spend the practice periods of one week in studying and practicing the two movement drills given in this lesson, reviewing each day everything that has gone before. Pupils in the sixth, seventh, and eighth years, and in high schools classes should be able to progress more rapidly. It is not

1) Berris
2) Yoghurt
3) apples
4) Bannana.

safe to say how rapidly, as that depends upon the knowledge of the teacher, the mental caliber of the pupils, their interest in the work, the length of the daily lessons, and the amount of the right kind of outside practicing that pupils do.

No. 28

Study the accompanying illustration, number twenty-eight. Notice the direction in which the upper part of the penholder points, the distance between the elbow and the side, the self-supporting position of the body in the chair, and the distance of the eyes from the paper. Do not forget that the force that moves the hand and carries the pen along without bending the fingers is above the elbow. It is not located in the fingers, hand, wrist, or forearm.

The fingers hold the pen easily and firmly without pinching; the third and fourth fingers are bent backward and form the movable rest under the hand; neither the wrist nor side of the hand touches the paper, and the arm should rest all the time on the largest portion in front of and near the elbow.

If the paper you are using has lines eight inches long, divide the page in the center from left to right with a dot; then divide the halves in the center with other dots. Beginning at the left for the straight line drill, make one hundred downward strokes to the first quarter mark, and continue in the same manner for each quarter. Thus, four hundred downward strokes and, of course, an equal number of upward strokes should be made in the four sections extending across a line. See drill one; page nineteen.

COUNTING TO REGULATE MOTION

In developing light, uniform motion in class penmanship practice, counting is important. It makes the work more interesting, tones down the movement of the naturally nervous pupil, acts as a constant spur to the habitually slow boy or girl, and keeps the indolent student busy. In the oblique straight line and the oval exercises given in drill one, the downward strokes only should be counted. The other parts of the drills, being what are termed connective lines, are not counted.

ABOUT SPEED

Speed is so important in the development of good writing that it should receive close attention in all practice work until correct speed has become a habit. Too much speed is just as bad as too little. Correct speed forces a light, firm line; too little speed results in shaky tremulous lines; while excessive speed means irregular letter formation. If you develop a light, firm, elastic motion, and the proper degree of speed in straight line and oval making, you will find the work of the following lessons comparatively easy.

The straight line and oval exercises in drills one, two, and three should be made at a speed of two hundred downward strokes to a minute; one hundred in one-half a minute; and then move the paper.

The most convenient count for continuous straight line or oval exercises as given in drill two is 1, 2, 3, 4, 5, 6, 7, 8, 9, 10—1, 2, 3, 4, 5, 6, 7, 8, 9, 20—1, 2, 3, 4, 5, 6, 7, 8, 9, 30—1, 2, 3, 4, 5, 6, 7, 8, 9, 40—1, 2, 3, 4, 5, 6, 7, 8, 9, 50, continuing until two hundred has been reached. Until correct speed habits have been developed, the second hand of a watch should be used as a guide.

A few minutes in the right way are worth more than hours of practice in the wrong way.

LESSON 5

Drill 2

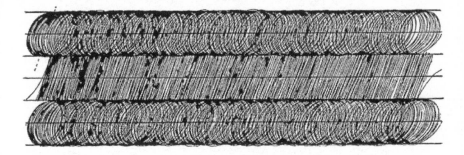

Begin this lesson with a review of position and movement, without the penholder. At least five minutes should be devoted to energetic practice of the straight line and oval drills in this way.

Do you see the dotted lines at the left in drill two? They are to show you the general direction in which the pen moves in making the downward strokes.

ABOUT SLANT

Slant needs no special study, but will take care of itself if the instructions have been studied and heeded. Especially is this true in relation to the position at the desk, the position of the paper and arms on the desk, the relation of each to the other, and the changing of the paper with the left hand, to keep it in the right position in regard to the desk, body, and arms. See diagrams—page eighteen.

If the position is correct, and if all downward strokes are made toward the center of the body, each pupil will develop uniform slant, though different pupils may develop individual slants. Following the same rules, and practicing at the same time under similar conditions, different slants result, because of the variations in length of arms, and other physical conditions. The degree of slant is not a matter of grave importance so long as each writer develops uniform slant in his own writing.

In drill two, see how many compact ovals you can make with one dip of ink, and try to develop a motion so light and elastic that you will soon be able to make from five hundred to a thousand, and one thousand or more on a line eight inches long.

Many young pupils have developed such control of muscular movement that they have made more than two thousand ovals with one dip of ink, in a space not more than eight inches long. Indeed, one boy of twelve made three thousand within the limits of a page eight inches across, maintaining a uniform speed of two hundred to a minute. The pen used was of the ordinary large, business variety.

Skill in oval making should be developed gradually from day to day, as two or three minutes at the beginning of each practice period are devoted to ovals. Never make ovals on the "back slant." Avoid this by pulling the strokes toward the center of the body.

LESSON 6

Each practice period should begin with a review of position, careful study of the arm, fingers, and penholding, and practice of the preceding movements without touching the pen to the paper. While going through these preliminary drills, the eyes should travel up and down the arm from finger-tips to elbow, and the pupils should be sure that the writing machine has been carefully adjusted, and is in perfect working order before the pen touches the paper. See that the arm is perfectly relaxed and that the wrist does not touch the desk.

PREPARATORY MOTION

Read the following carefully until thoroughly understood. It is of especial value to beginners. Before making the oval drill or attempting any part of it, move the pen in the air rapidly over the path of the first oval several times. While doing this, watch closely the movement of the muscles of the arm. While the pen is moving rapidly, and without checking its motion, let it strike the paper. The force thus gathered will compel light, quick action, break up finger motion, give smooth lines, and aid form building.

FORM BUILDING

The compact oval is the repeated form of a large capital O. Keep this constantly in mind, and learn at once to criticise it with special reference to the slant, width, and general formation of a capital O a little more than twice the size used in writing.

Mind and muscle must work in perfect harmony to secure the best results.

Before beginning the practice of any drill or letter, study its form closely, part by part, and as a complete whole. In what direction does the pen move to make the first line? See that the pen moves in that direction before coming in contact with the paper. Be sure that the speed is neither too fast nor too slow, but such as will make two hundred complete ovals to a minute. Do not guess about the speed, but use a watch.

If the oval is too wide, it is because of too nearly circular motion, and you should use more of the forward and backward motion of the straight line exercise. If too narrow, it is because too much of the straight line motion was used, and the movement should be more nearly circular. Remember the connection between mind, muscle, and motion.

When the oval is too narrow, repeat to yourself, "Wider, wider, rounder, rounder, rounder, rounder," until it is wide enough. If the oval presents a back slant appearance when finished, it is because the downward strokes were made toward the right elbow instead of the center of the body.

On the other hand, if the oval slants too much, it is because the downward strokes were made toward the left shoulder instead of the center of the body—always providing that instructions relating to position have been strictly followed.

Drill 3

When pupils make the ovals fairly well, they are ready to begin to apply muscular movement to words and sentences. The ovals given above are twelve-sixteenths of an inch high, and the letters in the word "mine" (called minimum letters) are about one-twelfth as high, or one-sixteenth of an inch. Thus, these ovals are twelve times as high as the minimum letters; therefore little force is required to make a minimum letter, compared with the muscular effort used in making ovals. To make the m and n round at the top, the over-motion must be used, while to make the connective lines of the i and e the use of the under-motion is necessary. In the words "uses" and "sell" the under-motion is used in forming the, first lines in all letters as well as in connective lines. The speed should be such as will permit good formation, and produce sharp, clear-cut lines.

Good practice speed for these words is "mine," eighteen; "uses," twenty: and "sell," twenty-two, to the minute. These words should be practiced now until they can be written well, and should be reviewed frequently. Practicing them at this stage with muscular movement will give students confidence and should encourage them to use, constantly, muscular movement in all written work. Other easy words may be selected from the Manual and practiced occasionally. It is a distinct advantage to study frequently at this stage lessons 15, 16, 17, 19, 20, and 32, and to practice drills 13, 14, 15, 17, 18, and 33.

LESSON 7

Drill 4

Begin, as usual, with careful study of the writing machine, adjust it carefully and test the movement. Then practice the two-space compact oval in drill three.

In drill four the special object is to develop a uniform, continuous motion. Preparatory to the first oval, the movement should be tested by carrying the pen rapidly in the air, the arm resting, and the hand in a good writing position. Without checking the motion, the pen should be brought to the paper, thus forcing it to make sharp, clean-cut lines. In passing from one oval to another, the pen should be lifted from the paper at the base line without checking the motion, should swing below the base line to the right and to the beginning of the next oval, a uniform speed being maintained throughout. Thus, the motion is continuous and no shaky lines are possible. Finish the final oval in each group with an upward right curve as shown in the drill. Move the paper with the left hand after each group of six.

Pupils should study the above instructions in connection with the oval practice until fully understood. These instructions are important, having a direct bearing upon the practice of capital letters.

Drill 5

Drill five is what we term a forcing movement drill, and is one of the best for the beginner to practice.

In the direct traced oval make six revolutions to a count of "1, 2, 3, 4, 5, 6," lifting the pen at the base line on the sixth count without checking the motion and swinging it in the air to the beginning stroke of the capital A. Thus the pupil will be impelled from a slow, lagging movement to one that is elastic and rapid. The form may not be entirely satisfactory at first, but it will improve rapidly if this process is continued long enough and frequently repeated.

The rate of speed should be about twenty complete traced ovals and as many capitals to the minute.

Before beginning to practice, count the ovals and letters. There are seven of each. You are expected to make the same number on a line of equal length.

LESSON 8—Drill 6

Assume correct position; practice the movement without, and then with, the penholder. Be sure that you are using exactly the right movement, and practice the two-space compact ovals two or three minutes at the rate of two hundred to a minute. (Drill three.)

When two lines are connected in an angle, a positive stop at the point of connection is necessary. This principle applies to the top of capital A where the upward and the last downward strokes are joined. This stop is such a small fraction of a second in duration that it can hardly be detected. Without the stop at the top of capital A, a loop will be made. To emphasize this stop in connection with capital A, the following conversational count has been developed. "You stop, you stop, at the top, you stop, every time, at the top. How long do you stop at the top? Not long, but you stop, every time, at the top. What for, what for, what for? Oh! To close them up, to close them up, to close them up," and repeat. Other conversational counts that may be used with capital A are, "Roll the arm, on the muscle; see it roll, on the muscle; slide the hand, on the fingers, see them slide, over the paper, make them glide." Make your letters the same size as in the drill, and begin each letter as the pen moves downward. Make capital A in groups of five, and move the paper a little to the left after each of the first two groups as indicated by the check mark. When the third group of five has been finished, move the paper to the right to its correct position for beginning a line. Learning to move the paper in this and in other drills is very important. There are three groups of five, making fifteen letters to a line in drill six, and five lines, seventy-five letters, should be made in a minute.

The dotted line between the first and second letters shows the path over which the pen should move without touching the paper, in passing from one letter to the next. A count of ten should be used in each group of five, and the count for each line should be 1-2, 3-4, 5-6, 7-8, 9-10, move the paper, 1-2, 3-4, 5-6, 7-8, 9-10, move the paper, 1-2, 3-4, 5-6, 7-8, 9-10, move the paper. In beginning every practice period hereafter, your program should be the two-space compact oval, one minute—two hundred ovals, and capital A, at a speed that will produce at least sixty-five and very soon seventy-five in a minute. For the present, three minutes could very profitably be spent in repeating the capital A with an easy, swinging, rhythmic motion. Select your best capital and compare it with the models giving close attention to size, slant, width, distance between letters, and the beginning and finishing lines.

If muscular movement is taught to pupils of the first and second year primary classes according to the Palmer Method plan, they will enter the third year of their school life well prepared to use the movement in all their Writing. If pupils in classes from the third to the eighth year inclusive have copies of this Manual, study it closely, and follow it absolutely in daily practice under teachers who have mastered the lessons before attempting to teach them, rapid improvement will be evident from week to week, and the ideal in rapid, easy, legible writing will soon be attained.

LESSON 9—Drill 7

Do not neglect the compact oval practice; one line across the paper will no doubt be enough if very compact.

The method of practice in drill seven should be the same as in capital A, drill five. After each traced oval, lift the pen while in motion, swinging it below the base line and around to the beginning point of capital O without checking it. Drive the pen rapidly and bring the muscles of the arm into active play. First make ten revolutions for the traced oval, gradually decreasing the number to six; count six for the ovals and two for each capital O.

Drill 8

This capital O is very popular with many excellent business penmen and teachers of modern writing. Study the letter and make a mental photograph of it. Note particularly the curves of the left and the right sides; also the loop at the top, its general direction and size.

In finishing O the final stroke should be pushed upward. If it is pulled downward it will too nearly resemble A.

Capital O should be made at thc rate of seventy or more to a minute. Count 1-2 for each O.

LESSON 10

Devote the time of this lesson to a general review of the preceding lessons.

LESSON 11—Drill 9

The plan of practice for drill nine should be the same as for drills five and seven. The count should be 1, 2, 3, 4, 5, 6,—1, 2, and repeat. No matter what may precede capital C, when the pen comes in contact with the paper in the beginning line it must move downward in the direction of a left curve.

Drill 10

How many are there on a line? Count them. Swing the pen in the path of a C several times before making the first letter; in fact, aim before you shoot. Lift the pen from the paper while in motion in finishing a capital; continue the motion with the pen in the air and bring it to the paper to begin the next capital—all without checking the motion. Make about seventy letters to the minute. Count 1-2 for each C.

LESSON 12

Drill 11

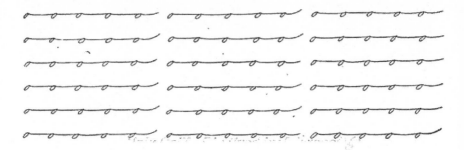

See instructions for drill eleven on following page.

Hereafter, each lesson should begin with practice of the compact two-space oval, drill three, drill six, and drill eleven, and there should be frequent reviews of the other drills so far practiced.

In the large oval drill and its modifications in capitals A, O, and C, the motion has been mainly forward and backward, while that used in the connected small o drill is mainly toward the right, developing the lateral movement. If too much driving force from above the elbow is used, the letter will be too large. If the position is just right, the least possible force will drive the hand far enough to form the o. The line connecting the letters should be as nearly straight as is possible to make it at the required speed. If too pronounced an under-curve is used in the connective lines the result will be a form more nearly resembling small a than o.

In this style of writing, small o and letters in its class should be one-sixteenth of an inch high. The letter in this drill is of that height, and it should be used as a basis of comparison in determining the height of the other minimum letters a, c, e, i, m, n, r, s, u, v, w, and x. Small r and s may be made one-fourth higher than the other letters in the minimum class.

Wherever there is an angular connection as in closing small o at the top, there must be a checking of the motion at that point; in fact, a stop. The closing of o is so quickly done that the stop can hardly be seen even by the closest observer.

To the Teacher: In connection with this drill we urge teachers to use a conversational count. In passing from desk to desk, criticise the work in correct rhythm. Suppose one student is making o too large, another not closing it at the top, another using a slow, dragging movement, another making a narrow, flat letter, and still another bending over his desk too far. The criticisms would be as follows: "Make it smaller, make it smaller; close it up, close it up; you stop, at the top, you stop, you stop, every time, at the top. How long? Not long; but you stop, every time, at the top. Slide along, slide along; round o, round o; sit up, sit up." Each criticism or admonition may be repeated until the error has in a measure been corrected. The influence will not be lost upon the rest of the pupils, but those who have been making the same errors will almost unconsciously show marked improvement.

A speed of ninety or more to a minute should be developed

and maintained. Ninety in a minute is by no means fast, but, while permitting good form, it is fast enough to force light motion.

In drill eleven, there are three groups of five letters in a line, and there are six lines in the drill, making ninety letters. These should be made in a minute, and that should be the practice speed. As in capital A, the plan is to make each group to a count of ten, and then move the paper. For an entire line the count would be 1-2, 3-4, 5-6, 7-8, 9-10, move the paper, 1-2, 3-4, 5-6, 7-8, 9-10, move the paper, 1-2, 3-4, 5-6, 7-8, 9-10, move the paper. The conversational count may be fitted nicely to the rhythm of the count of ten. Hereafter, drill eleven should be practiced with the two-space compact oval, and drill six at the beginning of each practice period.

LESSON 13

Make this a general review lesson.

The Palmer Method is a text-book on practical writing. The instructions should be studied and followed.

SPECIAL STUDIES OF THE CAPITALS, SMALL

LETTERS, AND FIGURES

ABCDEFGHIJKLM

NOPQRSTUVWXYZ

abcdefghijklmnop

qrstuvwxyz 1234567890.

Pupils who have studied and followed the explanations, suggestions, and instructions so far, will have sufficient control of the muscular movement to master easily the letters on this page.

Those who have not been thorough in studying the instruction and practicing the drills should review. Nothing less than failure can follow superficial study.

The capitals, small letters, and figures are given at this point for convenient reference, and an effort should be made hereafter to employ these forms in all the written work.

One lesson each week should be devoted to special study and practice of the capitals until they are mastered.

Capitals, small letters, and figures will all be taught thoroughly in the following lessons.

**A few minutes in the right way are worth more than
hours of practice in the wrong way.**

LESSON 14—Drill 12

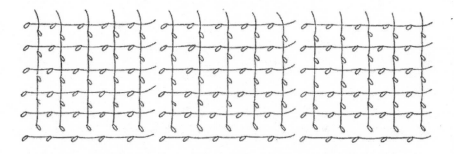

Cross line practice is very helpful in developing light, elastic,
gliding motion. First make the letters on the lines; then turn
the paper and make them across.

LESSON 15

MORE ABOUT COUNTING

In writing, as in music, regularity of movement is an
important factor. A jerky, spasmodic motion is to be avoided,
and successful teachers of writing have found that some
method to mark the time of making parts of letters is helpful.
Some use a metronome, some a chalk box and a ruler, others
musical instruments; but we prefer that wonderful machine,
the human voice, and a process of counting to fit the letters.
In individual home practice the counting process is of as

much value as in the school-room, and pupils should learn to use it.

When a letter is poorly made, it. may be due to one or all of four causes—first, the position may be poor; second, the muscles may be rigid, preventing easy action; third, the mind may not have a good picture of the form; and fourth, movement direction may be wrong. As an example, when small m and n are made too sharp at the top, it is because there is not enough over-motion.

The special object of drill thirteen is to develop the over-motion for m and n. As you practice this drill, count 1, 2, 3, 4, 5, 6, 7, 8, 9, 10, for each section, or use a verbal count as follows: Over, over, over, over, over, light, light, light, light, light. In the first line the exercise should occupy one-half the space between ruled lines; and in the second, the height should be the same as small o, one-sixteenth of an inch.

Drill 13

Remember that the larger part of the right arm just in front of the elbow, should rest on the desk, and the third and fourth fingers of the right hand be bent well under; that the position of the pen in the hand must be comfortable and the right arm well out from the side. Now push the hand forward and backward to test the freedom and movement power. If the muscles move easily, let the pen touch the paper, moving lightly and rapidly. About fourteen completed sections of the first line should be made in a minute and sixteen of the second.

LESSON 16

Drill 14

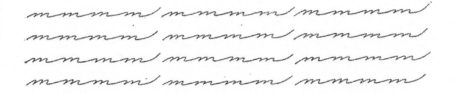

Test the movement by tracing the first stroke in the air. Start the motion below the base line, and as the pen moves rapidly upward let it strike the paper at the beginning point. Drive the pen through the exercise rapidly and lightly. Make four connected m's before lifting the pen, and three such groups across a line. You will make the letters too large, irregular, and awkward at first, and will have trouble with the union (connecting lines), but keep right on. Make the four lines in a minute and move the paper after each group. As taught in drill thirteen, lesson fifteen, the parts of small m are made with over-motion, but to use an over-motion between letters would give no connective line and hence no dividing line between the letters. Keep in mind as you practice, that the over-motion makes the parts of m, and that the opposite or under-motion forms the connecting lines. You may count 1, 2, 3; or slide, 2, 3; or over, over, under. Drill fourteen should be practiced a minute or more at the beginning of each practice period. Four drills have now been suggested for use at the beginning of every practice period. They should be practiced, not only in the beginning stages, but until the entire course has been mastered. These drills furnish the very best movement exercises, and at the same time give the right kind of practice in form building. Students who thoroughly master them in size, form, and speed application will find the remaining drills easy. As it teaches the correct use of the under-motion in connecting letters, small m is perhaps the most important of the four.

LESSON 17

From his point each lesson should start with the compact two-space oval; drill eleven, small o; and drill fourteen, small m. It will pay to devote from three to five minutes of each practice period to these three drills.

Drill 15

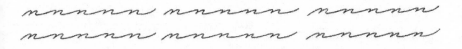

For small m, a count of three is used; and in n, a count

of two. Thus, the count for drill fifteen will be 1, 2, 1, 2, 1, 2, 1, 2, etc., or for five connected letters, 1-2, 3-4, 5-6, 7-8, 9-10. The speed should be the same relatively as in the small m drill.

LESSON 18

Drill 16

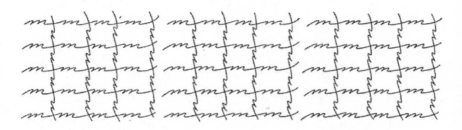

Make the small m in groups of four, three groups to a, line, and five or more rows; then turn the paper and make groups of small n. Make frequent comparisons with the drill as you practice.

LESSON 19

Drill 17

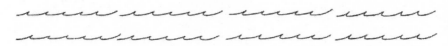

Smali i being made entirely with an under-motion, has a sharp point at the top. Count 1, 2, 3, 4, 5, for each group; make the downward as light as the upward strokes and try to make them equal distances apart.

Drill 18

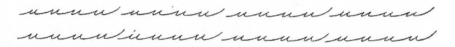

A space in width is the distance between the points of small u. This is sometimes called a lateral space. For each group of four connected letters, count 1-2, 3-4, 5-6, 7-8.

Drill 19

Extend small i about two and one-half times its height, cross with a short horizontal line, and the result will be small t. An effort should be made to bring the upward and downward strokes of small t together at the top, but if a very short narrow loop is sometimes made as a result of rapid movement, it will not conflict with legibility. The small t should always be a little shorter than the small l and its companions, b, h, k, and f. The practice speed for t in groups of five is twenty groups, or one hundred letters, to the minute. There is no special value in this letter as a movement drill, but a little practice of it in group formation will be an aid to its mastery.

As you gain more control of the muscular movement,

you should become more skillful in its application, and the result should be constant improvement in form, spacing, and uniformity of size. Use your eyes constantly, comparing your letters with the drills you are trying to imitate; do your best, and rapid improvement is sure to follow.

LESSON 20

After the usual practice of the compact two-space oval and the small m and n review lesson nineteen.

Drill 20

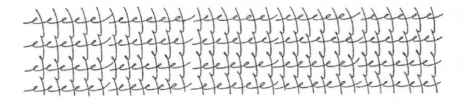

The count for small e in groups of five, is 1, 2, 3, 4, 5. Try to make the letter but one-sixteenth of an inch high. For purposes of comparison, it would be well occasionally to make rows of small o's and m's on lines close to your small e drills. The three letters should be of the same height. Making small e in groups of five, twenty-eight groups, or one hundred and forty letters, should be made in a minute.

LESSON 21

Drill 21

Annum Annum Annum Annum
Annum Annum Annum Annum

Wrong practice will lead you in the wrong direction: The instructions tell you how to practice.

Number twenty-one is our first word drill with a capital. Do not neglect the study of the motion and its applications to form.

Write fourteen or more words to a minute, and do not let them occupy more space than the copies. In orill six the final line in capital A drops below the base line. This is done to give a rhythmic movement drill. In writing words beginning with capital A it is better to connect the last line with the small letters following, as in the second line in drill twenty-one.

LESSON 22

Drill 22

Common Common Common Common
Common Common Common Common

Write fourteen words in a minute. Write a few lines and then compare your work with the drill. Review often.

LESSON 23

Drill 23

[cursive handwriting drill: "Omen" repeated across two lines]

Be sure that the motion is oval in starting capital O. Trace the letter with the pen in the air. Let the pen strike the paper when moving rapidly downward.

If all conditions are favorable and the movement is free, about sixteen of these should be written in a minute.

LESSON 24

Drills 24 and 25

[cursive handwriting drill exercises]

Study the upper line closely, and notice particularly that the nine exercises at the right are the enlarged form of an inverted figure six.

Fix clearly in your mind the direction of the moving pen as it comes into contact with the paper in making the beginning loop. Do not make this loop larger than it is in the drill. For business writing it would be better to make a dot than a large loop. Energetic practice of the drill at the left in the first line will help to develop the right motion. In that part of the drill a count of 1, 2, 3, 4, 5, should be used. In the nine forms at the right in the first line, the count may be 1-2, down over; or down, over; or one stop for each; but each form should stop abruptly at the base line in a blunt stroke.

As this form is used for the beginning of twelve capitals, it should be thoroughly studied and practiced now, and frequently reviewed.

In the lower line, observe that five drills extend across the page, with ten parts in each drill; with the paper held in the right position, the downward strokes should be made toward the center of the body, and the over-motion is applied in making the turns at the top. The count should be 1, 2, 3, 4, 5, 6, 7, 8, 9, 10, and sixteen completed exercises should be made to the minute.

Turn to page twenty-nine and pick out the twelve capitals in which the inverted figure six is used. Use this style hereafter in beginning those capitals.

This is a lesson that should be reviewed frequently.

LESSON 25

You should not forget the usual three to five minute practice period devoted to the compact oval, and the small o and m drills.

Drills 26 and 27

Study capitals M and N closely before trying to make them. Compare their parts in relation to slant, height, and width. Your attention is particularly directed to the finishing lines in M and N. Dropping this line below the base, and lifting the pen without stopping the motion, forces freedom, continues the rotary motion and develops an automatic movement preceding and following each letter, so that the motion is continued, even when you are not actually forming the letters.

The capital M should be made in a count of 1, 2, 3, 4, at the rate of thirty a minute, and capital N in a count of 1, 2, 3, at the rate of forty a minute.

LESSON 26

Review lessons twenty-four and twenty-five.

LESSON 27

Perhaps you have forgotten something; perhaps you were about to begin your practice of drill twenty-eight without the review of the compact oval, and small o and m. If so, do not forget again.

Drill 28

Moon Moon Moon Moon Moon Moon Moon Moon Moon Moon Moon Moon

In penmanship, constant repetition is essential, and in connection with drill twenty-eight the best results will be secured by practicing the word several minutes. We prefer to have pupils at first use the style of capital given in the first line, in which the finishing stroke is carried below the base, and the pen lifted from the paper before the small letters are made. Later the final stroke in capital M may be connected directly with any small letters following, as in the second line. You are expected to write six words on a line, as in the copy, writing from fourteen to seventeen a minute.

To the Teacher: If you have studied the lessons in advance, have practiced the different drills and mastered them before giving them to your pupils, a good plan to follow in word-practice is sometimes to sit at your desk, or a pupil's desk writing the words with them and spelling as you write. Thus: M-o-o-n, M-o-o-n. This will enable you to help your boys and girls to master the correct speed, and to secure uniform motion.

Never attempt to use the count for individual letters when practicing words; it is confusing.

LESSON 28

Drill 29

Noon Noon Noon Noon Noon Noon
Noon Noon Noon Noon Noon Noon

Make a few lines of capital N as a movement drill before practicing the word Noon. Repeated letters and words should always be considered movement drills. Strive for a firmer, lighter motion constantly. Examine all letters and words practiced with special reference to firm, smooth lines, their direction, size, distances between letters, height and width of the different parts, connecting lines, the finishing lines in the final letters, and every little detail.

Write from fifteen to eighteen words a minute.

LESSON 29

FOR STUDY AND COMPARISON

aaaaa aaaaa aaaaa
A ddddd ddddd ddddd
q q g gggg ggggg ggggg ggggg
ggggg ggggg ggggg ggggg

Small a is, in the main, a reduced copy of capital A, and the first parts of small d, g, and q are identical with it. Fix the resemblance in the mind; it will help you. In business writing it is best to make the looped small d. It is just as legible as the stem and can be made more rapidly. The loop below the base line in small g should be made without finger motion. We favor the blunt style of small g and y at the end of words, and this ending should be shorter than the loop. Fix in your mind the length of this abbreviated g. Small q is a little shorter below the base line than g. The g ending bluntly below the base line, is just like the figure nine.

Drill 30

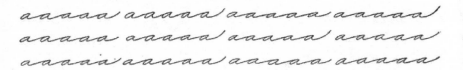

It will pay you to practice the small a drill a great deal. Try to make a half-dozen or more lines of letters as small and as uniform as the copy. Students should not forget to study the copy constantly and to make frequent comparisons of their work with it. A count of 1, 2, should be used for each small a, and in connecting five letters it is a good plan to count 1-2, 3-4, 5-6, 7-8, 9-10.

Small a in groups of five should be made at the rate of seventy a minute.

LESSON 30

Drill 31

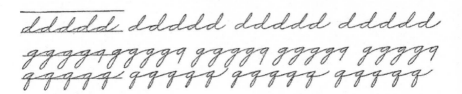

Reckoning small o, one-sixteenth of an inch high, as one space, small g should extend three spaces, or three-sixteenths of an inch below the baseline, while the loop of q and abbreviated g should extend two spaces below.

The loop of d extends about two and one-half spaces above the base.

Writing which is good in other respects is often spoiled in the written page because the loops are too long, extending into the lines above and below.

The count for each letter in groups of five should be 1-2, 3-4, 5-6, 7-8, 9-10, and the speed should be: small d, from sixty-five to seventy; g, from sixty to sixty-five; and q, about fifty to the minute.

Are you studying the instructions? They tell you just how to succeed.

LESSON 31

Drill 32

gadding gadding gadding gadding

Review lesson thirty before you study and practice this drill.

If you use your eyes to good advantage, you will see that the first g begins one space above the base line, there being no initial line starting from the base; also that the first parts of small g and d are of the same height as a, o, m, and n. to which special reference has already been made. Practice speed, twelve words in a minute.

LESSON 32

The basis of the extended loop letters. b, f, h, and k, is small l. These five letters should extend the same distance above the base line. The practice of small l should be thorough now, and it should be reviewed often. In fact, it would be well to add it to the group of compact ovals, and small m's and o's, to be practiced at the beginning of each lesson.

Height—Reference has already been made to one-sixteenth of an inch as representing a space in height for the minimum (one-space) letters a, c, e, i, m, n, o, u, v, w, and x. The small r and s are in the same class, but are made a quarter space higher than the others.

69

These minimum letters should always be used as a standard of one-space measurement to regulate the height of all other small letters. On that basis small l should be four spaces—four-sixteenths, or one-fourth of an inch high. As there are six-sixteenths of an inch between the ruled lines in the practice paper generally used, and in all the Palmer Method practice paper, there should be two-sixteenths (one-eighth) of an inch between the top of the loop and the ruled line above.

It should be remembered that a space in height is the height of the minimum letters in the style you are practicing. As an example, in copybooks used in former years, the one-space letters were one-eighth of an inch, or twice as high as in these lessons. The loop letters were three spaces, or three-eighths of an inch high, which is two-sixteenths of an inch higher than the loops in these lessons.

Movement Used—In business writing, all loops below the line should be made with pure muscular movement. In making those above the line, the fingers should be relaxed, and as the arm slides forward, a slight extension of the fingers will help to make the upper part of the loop. The combination of the two movements is perfectly natural to most hands, and little encouragement need be given to the use of the fingers. The student must guard against using much of it. Keep an eye on your wrist to see that it moves forward and backward in unison with the other movements. Under no circumstances allow the fleshy part of the hand in front of the wrist to touch the paper.

Cautions—You will find your first difficulty in getting enough curve on the upward stroke. A half hour's determined practice will do much to overcome this. Keep the paper at such an angle as will make the downward strokes straight toward the middle of the body. Above all, preserve unity in height; in slant and in spacing. Do not shade.

Drill 33

There is a slight check in the motion on the downward strokes, but no pause at the base line. After a little practice, loops as good as the above should be made at the rate of from one hundred to one hundred and twenty-five to the minute. The count in groups of five is 1, 2, 3, 4, 5—one for each letter.

LESSON 33

Drill 34

More study, more practice. Study and practice should be constant companions in developing good writing. One without the other will lead to one-sided results. Don't be one-sided.

Drill thirty-four offers good movement practice. Close observation will indicate just how it is done. The small traced oval is about one-half the capital in height, and the upper loop is also one-half the entire height of the letter. If you have a sharp eye and a responsive mind, you have been able to grasp these details without any suggestions, and you have gone further. You have noted the curve in the main downward stroke, the flatness of the lower loop on the base line, and the dropping of the finishing stroke below the base.

Six is the count for the traced oval and two for L, as follows, 1-2-3-4-5-6, 1-2. The count of 1-2, for the capital L should be a little slower than for the ovals. This exercise should be made ten times on a line, in groups of five, and two lines, or twenty exercises a minute.

A few minutes in the right way are worth hours of practice in the wrong way.

Drill 35

Swing for the L, swing for the L, swing for the L. In other words, study the letter closely, and swing the pen in its direction a few times before making it. The first line starts about one-half the distance from the base to the top, and dips under; the upper loop is one-half the entire length of the letter; the lower loop rests on the base line; and the finishing line is carried below the base. This letter makes one of the best movement drills so far given. After each group of five the paper should be moved.

The count is 1-2, for each letter, or slide two, or slide L, or swing L. From fifty to fifty-five should be made in a minute.

LESSON 34

Review lesson thirty-three.

Drill 36

Lanning Lanning Lanning Lanning

Study, practice, and compare.

Begin small a at the top just as it is in drill thirty; make the abbreviated g short below the base line, and be sure to write

73

four words to a line. Practice speed, ten to twelve words a minute.

LESSON 35

Drill 37

Lulling Lulling Lulling Lulling

Write two lines and then make careful comparisons with the models. Are your small l's shorter than the capitals; are both l's the same height; and do they cross one space above the base? Compare slant, the parts of letters and letters complete. Study the spacings between the letters, and try to show improvement in each line. Practice speed, the same as for drill thirty-six.

You cannot fail, if you study the instructions and follow them.

LESSON 36

Drill 38

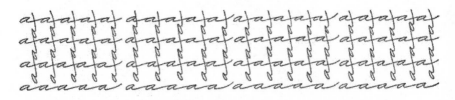

Small a should be reviewed frequently as a movement drill.

Drill 39

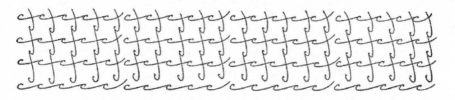

The first part of small a serves as the foundation of small c. In making connective lines, an over-motion must be used. If an under-motion is used from the ending of one c to the dot at the top of the next, there will be a loop, and the letter will be too large. After making a few lines, compare the height of c with o, a, m, and n. You will, of course, frequently compare with the copy. The count is 1-2, 3-4, 5-6, 7-8, 9-10; or dot over, dot over, dot over, dot over, dot over, for each group of five. The speed should be sixteen groups of five, or eighty letters a minute.

LESSON 37

Drill 40

The small r given in the first line in drill forty cannot be made at a high rate of speed, as the form requires a checking of movement at the top to form the shoulder. Study the parts of the letter shown before the first completed form.

The form in the second line can be made at much higher speed, and, while somewhat difficult to learn, is much easier in execution when mastered. The first part of it is just like the first part of small m or n. The downward stroke is retraced to a point about one-fourth of a space above the first part; a stop (hardly noticeable) and a dot are made before the swinging curve to the next letter. If the connective lines between letters of this style are made with too much under-curve, perhaps touching the base line, they will more nearly resemble small x than r. Guard against this fault.

Close study of the form while practicing will be necessary. After its mastery, ninety connected letters to the minute will be a good rate of speed. Unquestionably, the first few trials will be discouraging, but faithful practice will be rewarded. Stick to it.

Eighteen groups of five should be made to the minute.

Drill 41

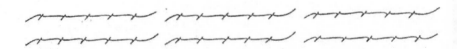

The count for this small r in drill forty-one for each group of five is 1-2, 3-4, 5-6, 7-8, 9-10; or one-dot, two-dot, three-dot, four-dot, five-dot; or one-stop, two-stop, three-stop, four-stop, five-stop. A conversational count similar to that in small o, drill eleven, may be used to advantage in small r, thus—You-stop, you-stop, you-stop, you-stop, at-the-top. How long, do you stop, at the top? Not long, but you stop, every time at the top. What for, what for, what for? To make a dot, to make a dot, to make a dot, etc.

Drill 42

The rate of practice speed in this drill should be twenty or more words to the minute.

Drill 43

There is no initial line before small o; it begins at the top.

LESSON 38

As before mentioned, small r and s are companion letters, and both may be made one-fourth higher than other letters of the minimum class; not because of any technical rule, but rather because it generally is agreed that they look better so made. Small s should be pointed, not looped, at the top, and entirely closed on the base line. Be sure to use just the right amount of under-curve in the beginning stroke, and the width will depend upon the amount of curve in the last part. Practice, study, and compare.

Drill 44

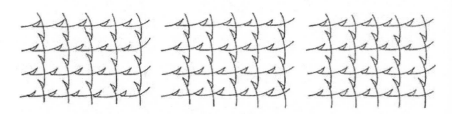

The count for each group of five is 1-2, 3-4, 5-6, 7-8, 9-10. A conversational count similar to that given in the small o drill could be used to advantage; thus, swing one, swing two, swing three, swing four, swing five; or curve one, curve two, curve three, curve four, curve five. Nearly or quite seventeen groups of five should be made to the minute.

LESSONS 39, 40, 41, 42, AND 43

At least five lessons at this point should be devoted to reviewing all the lessons that have gone before.

THE FREQUENCY OF REVIEWS

To Teachers: Assuming that teachers of the Palmer Method master the lessons in their order before attempting to teach them, they are to decide when lessons and drills have not been mastered and need reviewing. Without knowing the pupils and seeing their daily work in penmanship, it would hardly be possible for the author to decide with unerring accuracy, when they should review.

LESSON 44

Drill 45

The first two parts of small w form u. As explained in lesson nineteen, the distance between the points in small u represents a lateral (running) space. Keeping this space in mind, carry the third or finishing part of small w one-half space to the right of the second, or finishing point in small u. The connecting stroke is slightly curved.

Eighteen or twenty groups of three should be made to the minute and the count for each letter is 1, 2, 3; 1, 2, 3; 1, 2, 3; or one, two, dot; one, two, dot; one, two, dot.

Drill 46

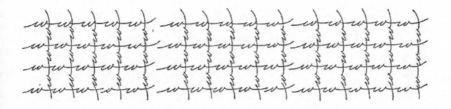

LESSON 45

Drill 47

Small x is simple in construction. Study closely before practicing it. The crossing may be made either upward or downward. In writing a word containing it, complete the word before crossing the letter. Make the crossing short.

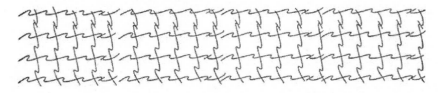

Drill 48

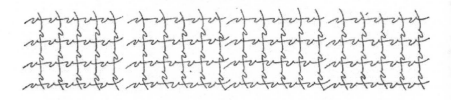

LESSON 46—Drill 49

The first part of small v is the same as the first part of small x, and it is ended with the form used in finishing small w. Don't close this letter at the top. It must be left open. Count 1-2, 3-4, 5-6, 7-8, 9-10, for each group of five letters.

Drill 50

waive waive waive waive waive waive

LESSON 47—Drill 51

hhhhh hhhhh hhhhh hhhhh
hhhhh hhhhh hhhhh hhhhh

The loop in h is small l, brought to the base in a straight line on the main slant, the second part is one section of small m. Notice that the first and last parts of small h meet on the base in a point. Study until you see just how it is done.

A count of 1-2, should be used for one h, and a count of 1-2, 3-4, 5-6, 7-8, 9-10, for a group of five. From fourteen to fifteen groups of five should be made in a minute.

Study an inverted h, and if correctly made you will see that in that position it is small y. At this point it would be well to study and practice small y. Count 1-2, 3-4, 5-6, 7-8, 9-10, for each group of five.

Drill 52

LESSON 48

Review lessons forty-seven and forty-eight, and then give attention to the following.

Drill 53

hill hill hill hill hill hill hill
hull hull hull hull hull hull
hilly hilly hilly hilly hilly hilly

The practice speed should be twenty or more of the first two words and sixteen or more of the third word to the minute. Guard against making h higher than 1. All loop letters above the base should be the same length.

LESSON 49

THE REVERSE OVAL AND ITS APPLICATION

An application of the reverse oval motion is made in forming capital J. The reverse oval, it must be understood, begins with an upward stroke on the left side. Before attempting capital J, make reverse ovals four or five minutes, and if the movement is then light and uniform, the copy may be safely practiced. The oval is used as the developing and stroke on the left side. driving force.

Drill 54

Make the oval to a count of six, lift the pen from the paper at the top, and without checking the motion swing the pen in its natural course above the paper, to the right and below the base to the point of contact with the paper in starting the letter. Do not stop the motion, but strike the paper in an upward course at full speed for the beginning stroke of J. If the explanation of applied motion is not fully understood, study until it is, and then fill at least a half page with the copy.

Do not neglect the form, but note carefully the following points: J should begin with an upward stroke from a point just below the base line; the turn at the top should be round; the upper part should be a little longer than the lower part, and twice its width.

LESSON 50—Drill 55

If slant is troublesome, study and practice this drill faithfully.

Drill 56

James James James James James James

This copy is given as a drill on both movement and form. From the beginning stroke of J to the finishing of small s the pen should not be lifted. Write the word from beginning to end with a steady, light and uniform movement. Eighteen or twenty words to the minute will be a fair rate of speed for practice.

LESSON 51

Drill 57

Make capital I, and continue with the reverse oval. The count should be two for I and six for th oval, as follows: 1, 2; 3, 4, 5, 0, 7, 8. Apply enough speed to make the lines smooth and clear-cut.

Drill 58

Question: Where and how does capital I begin? Answer: Below the base line with upward motion. Question: How wide is the upper part? Answer: A little less than half the width of the lower part. Question: How is it finished? Answer: With a full left curve and a dot at the end. Question: Where do the first upward and the first downward lines cross? Answer: At the height of small o. Question: What part of the space between the ruled lines is occupied by I? Answer: About three-fourths. You should analyze every letter you practice just as completely as is done in these questions and answers. Then you will have good mental pictures of the letters, will see at once when they are poorly made, and will make them well as soon as you have good control of the movement. Without the good mental picture, you will never write well, no matter how perfect your control of motive power may be.

With a count of 1, 2, for each letter, make forty-five or more to a minute.

Drill 59

To form the angle at the left, there must be a full stop in this style of capital I. It is hoped that you have remembered and tried to apply the instructions of an earlier lesson about stops in making all angular connections.

This is a particularly good style of capital I to use in beginning a word, as shown in the following drill. Count 1, 2, 3; or 1, 2, swing.

Drill 60

Ionian Ionian Ionian Ionian

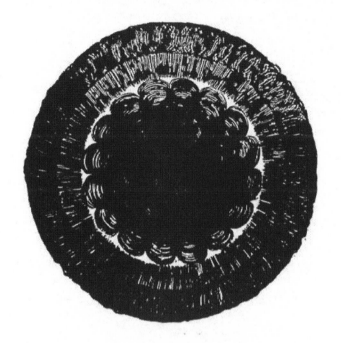

MOVEMENT DRILL DESIGN

IT is often a good plan to encourage students to give full play to their inventive and constructive ability in adapting the drills to different designs. Such work, however, should be done largely out of school hours. A great variety of such designs from schools where the Palmer Method is in use may be seen on the walls of the author's offices. In the drills mentioned are mainly used the straight line; compact, open and interlaced ovals, large and small; small m, n, e, o, c, l, h, and b. Among these designs are houses, carriages, crosses, battleships, and many curious designs for which we do not find names. Many are worked out in colored inks and the effect, on the whole, is pleasing.

Herewith we give a drill that is a favorite exercise with many teachers. Let the student use pencil outlines to indicate length of lines and width of ovals.

YOU CANNOT FAIL, IF YOU STUDY THE INSTRUCTIONS AND FOLLOW THEM

LESSONS 52 AND 53

Not forgetting or neglecting the two-space compact oval drill with which each lesson should start, the practice periods of two days might well be spent in study and practice of the letters on page 52.

LESSON 54—Drill 61

This copy furnishes all the movement drill necessary in beginning this lesson. Count ten for each drill, two for capital S, and eight for the reverse traced oval. About sixteen complete drills should be made to the minute. This drill is especially recommended to those who find the development of a light, quick movement difficult.

Drill 62

SSSSS SS SSS SSSSS

Study the curve of the first stroke; study the loop at the top, and give especial attention the fact that the loop (upper part of S) is one-half the entire length of the letter. With an easy, light movement make from forty-five to fifty letters to the minute. Count 1, 2, for each letter.

Drill 63

SSSS S SSSS SSSSS

The angular finishing stroke shown in drill sixty-three is very popular with many excellent teachers of business writing. Almost the same number of letters should be made in a minute as in drill sixty-two. Its practical feature is the direction taken by the finishing stroke, which may be joined to any letter following. Count 1, 2, swing; or 1, 2, 3, for each letter.

LESSON 55—Drill 64

Summit Summit Summit Summit

Write a page of this copy; more if you have sufficient time. A continuous steady movement should be used. Do not lift the pen from the beginning to the ending of the word.

LESSON 56

Drill 65

In this drill, capital G is made first to a count of three, and then, without lifting the pen, followed with six revolutions of the reverse traced oval. Make seventeen completed exercises in a minute. Count as follows: 1, 2-3, 4, 5, 6, 7, 8, 9.

Drill 66

Study the form of capital G closely before attempting to make it; be sure that you not only know when you make a poor letter, but that you know why it is poor. One bad stroke may spoil an otherwise good letter. Learn to locate the bad strokes. Make from forty to fifty letters to the minute. Count 1, 2, 3; or 1, stop, 3, for each letter.

Drill 67

This is a good business form. Special instruction is unnecessary. Use your eyes. Make as many as fifty in a minute.

Drill 68

The angular finishing stroke gives a connective line for any letter that may follow, and admits of joining the capitals for an extended drill as well. Coast 1, 2, for each letter, or 1-2, 3-4, 5-6, for each group of three. Make eighteen groups in a minute.

You aim before you shoot. You should study the instructions before you practice the drills.

LESSON 57—Drill 69

Nothing can be better at this stage of the work than easy words constantly repeated. Through a series of repetitions, strength in movement is developed, and faults are seen. Twelve or fourteen words to a minute should be the practice speed.

LESSON 58

CAUTION TO THE STUDENT

Never begin to practice until you are sure you know how. Languid, thoughtless practice should be avoided. Put ambition, put energy, put the fire of determined will behind your practice, and the results will be astonishing. Take advantage of all favorable conditions. Not only keep the muscles of the right arm in a relaxed condition, but guard against tension in any part of the body. Keep the side of the hand and the wrist free from the desk; keep the right arm well out from the side; keep the right hand in front of the eyes; keep a right angle at the right elbow, and remember that the propelling power is located above the right elbow. If you think you are in a good position for writing, test the movement without touching the pen to the paper, and study the conditions under which you are trying to work. Be sure you are right before you go ahead.

Drill 70

Not much movement drill of a special character is necessary in opening this lesson, the connected small p affording an excellent exercise. Study the form with care. Note particularly the point at the top, the loop below the base line, the length above and below the base, and the point where the left curve from below the base crosses the main line.

Sixty connected letters should be made to the minute. Make frequent comparisons and write a page.

The count for each group is 1-2, 3-4, 5-6, 7-8, 9-10.

Drill 71

pull pull pull pull pull pull

Average rate of speed, twenty words to the minute. If small l is difficult, turn to drill thirty-three, study the instructions, and practice small l as there presented.

Drill 72

pulling pulling pulling pulling

The practice speed should be fourteen words to a minute.

LESSON 59

Drill 73

PPPPP PPPPP PPPPP

Make a few imaginary letters as a preliminary movement drill before beginning active work. As will be seen, nearly all the main oval part is at the left of the beginning stroke. Count 1, 2, and repeat; or 1-2, 3-4, 5-6, 7-8, 9-10 for each group of five. Move the paper after each group of five. From fifty to sixty letters should be made to the minute. Make a full page and practice steadily, not spasmodically. This letter lends itself readily to a light, easy, swinging, and rhythmic movement. For that reason, it is an excellent movement drill, and the best style of capital P to adopt.

Drill 74

Also make a page of this letter. It is a good movement drill. Count three and be sure to join the last part to the first with a loop a little above the center of the letter. Forty-five good letters should be made to the minute. Count 1, 2, 3.

Drill 75

Count 1-2, 3-4, 5-6, 7-8, 9-10, for each group of five, and make twelve groups or sixty letters to the minute.

LESSON 60

Review lessons fifty-eight and fifty-nine.

Drill 76

Pippin Pippin Pippin Pippin

Write from ten to twelve words a minute, four to a line, eight inches long. This is a good movement drill if properly practiced.

LESSON 61—BUSINESS FIGURES

Nothing is more important to the average bookkeeper or office clerk than good figures. In many lines of accounting, thousands of business figures are made without the writing of a single word.

This, in a measure, is true in many branches of statistical work connected with railroad bookkeeping where headings are printed and page after page is filled with figures. The first requisite is legibility, and its importance cannot be emphasized too much. Letters in a word may be known by the context, but each figure must depend upon itself for legibility. It is very important, then, that each figure should be so formed that its netted value, in groups or by itself, cannot be mistaken.

AN OBJECT-LESSON, FOR STUDY

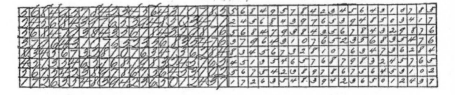

Through the adoption of the Palmer Method figures, made small and well within the spaces, the New England Telephone Co. has reduced errors of its employes to a minimum, and saved thousands of dollars a year.

Figures should be made small; students sometimes think that large figures are necessarily plainer, but such is not the case. Examine carefully the diagram. At the left are figures that are absolutely plain; on could not be mistaken for another, and yet their extreme size in the small spaces makes them difficult to read. At the right are the same figures, no more perfect, but not so large. Please note carefully that these, surrounded by white paper, and much smaller, are more legible, even at a distance, than the large figures at the left.

Students who have practiced in copy-books almost invariably make figures three or four times too large. Our models are large enough for ordinary use. If occasion demands, it will be easy to make them larger. One-eighth of an inch is perhaps high enough for ordinary figures, while in some places it will be an advantage to make them even smaller.

FOR STUDY

1 2 3 4 5 *1 2 3 4 5 6 7 8 9 0* *6 7 8 9 0*

HOW TO PRACTICE

In making figure one, draw the hand toward you with a quick light motion, sliding on the third and fourth fingers. Uniformity in the height and slant are the two important points to observe.

The development and application of a lateral oval motion will aid in the construction of figure two. In making it in class drill a count of three should be used, thus—one, two, three, one, two, three, etc., or dot, two, three.

Notice the exercise preceding, figure three in lesson sixty-five. The motion used in that exercise will produce a good figure if properly applied. One, two, three, or dot, two, three, is the count used. A count of three is used in figures four and five also, but for figures six, seven, and nine, use a count of two.

Several lessons should be given to drilling on the figures singly before grouping them, but as soon as the forms are mastered and the student can make them at a fair rate of speed, it is best to drill in miscellaneous order somewhat as follows: 1, 0, 2, 6, 9, 8, 5, 4, 3, 0, 9, 6, 7, 2, 2, 8, 9, 3, 5, 6, 9, 1, 5, 8, 6, 9, 5, 4, 6, 9, 3, 7, 8, etc. Na particular order is necessary, but the aim should be to repeat one as often as another.

LESSON 62

Drill 77

[handwriting drill: rows of looped practice strokes]

LESSON 63

Drill 78

[handwriting drill: rows of looped practice strokes]

It is truly interesting to watch the development and improvement in figure practice in a class where the work is well and systematically done. Two weeks should be devoted to this practice and there should be frequent reviews.

Some teachers place great emphasis upon the order of simplicity, but as a matter of fact, no two students will be able to agree on this and, since we are going to devote some time to drilling on each figure during a period of two weeks, there is little use in attempting any arrangement on such a basis. If there is a difference, the difficult figures should be given most practice.

LESSON 64

Drill 79

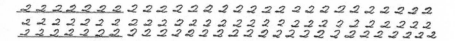

As soon as fair progress has been made in making figure two, an effort should be made to bring the rate of speed to seventy-five a minute. Count one, two, three, or dot, two, three, for each figure made in class practice.

LESSON 65

Drill 80

In the author's classes the method here presented of teaching figure 3 has proved more satisfactory than any other that he has tested. The motion produces the figure; learn this motion thoroughly. Count one, two, three, or dot, two, three, and make seventy figures a minute.

The Palmer Method is a text-book on practical writing. The Instructions should be studied, and followed.

LESSON 66

Drill 81

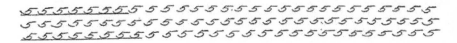

Figure five is in a large measure dependent upon the horizontal stroke at the top for its legibility. This horizontal line should be made last. Study the form as well as practice it. About seventy good figures should be made to the minute. This speed may be increased later. Count one, two, three.

LESSON 67

Drill 82

Seven extends below the base. Make this figure in a count of one, two, at the rate of about eighty-five to the minute.

LESSON 68

Drill 83

Four rests on the base line, and usually the last part extends above the first. Count one, two, three, and make from sixty to seventy a minute.

LESSON 69

Drill 84

The compound curve at the left on the first line in drill 84, and the arrow in the first figure show how 8 begins.

After a few minutes' drill on figure eight at a speed of sixty to seventy a minute, miscellaneous figures should be introduced. In class work these figures should be made from the dictation of the teacher, and the practice speed should be from ninety to one hundred figures to the minute. The author usually makes the figures on the blackboard as they are dictated to the class. A fairly rapid penman can make from one hundred to one hundred and twenty-five of these in a minute. Compare your figures with the copies and make all figures small and disconnected.

MISCELLANEOUS FIGURES FOR STUDY AND

PRACTICE

35567	4583746	175	564	325	762
43984	6237294	175	893	465	925
15678	35494453	264	429	395	763
34210	4672746	264	384	437	925
76301	94624955	264	565	625	925
27653	23544376	264	495	438	495
94378	10444472	329	346	965	925
62343	6134821	329	762	343	765
47837	24257699	329	925	925	348
62953	56473783	329	495	495	925
29435	4759292	525	348	643	925
43962	38967699	525	925	595	535

LESSON 70

Drill 85

SPECIAL POINTS TO OBSERVE

Capital E is made with an application of the oval motion, as developed in capitals O, A and C, the application varying but little.

The upper part of capital E is about one-third the entire height of the letter. The finishing oval should not exceed one-half the entire height, and the loop marking two-thirds the height of the letter points downward at about a right angle with the main slant.

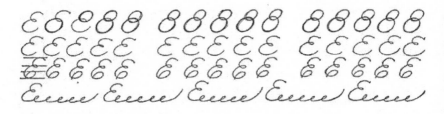

Practice the first row as a movement drill. Make the small (upper) oval first, and swing into the lower and larger oval without lifting the pen. Make five traced ovals for the upper, and the same for the lower part, thus permitting a count of ten for each completed exercise.

The abbreviated E in the second line is used by good business penmen more than any other, but the form used in the next line, finished with an oval, should be practiced and mastered. The count for each should be 1, 2, 3, or dot, 2, 3. From forty-five to fifty of the abbreviated form and but few less of the other should be made to the minute. Count the number of letters on a line, and make as many in the same space. The abbreviated capital E, followed with the small e, may be practiced as a movement drill to good advantage now and during future practice periods. The count for it is 1, 2, 3, 4, 5, 6, 7, or dot, 2, 3, 4, 5, 6, 7.

Review this lesson often until you make a good capital E.

It is not Palmer Method if the lines are tremulous. Study the instructions for speed requirements.

LESSON 71

Drill 86

The framework of capital B is clearly shown in the models below. The straight line starting at a point about three-fourths of the distance from the base is purely a guide line, a prop upon which the remainder rests. Without it, beginners make very feeble letters. Although usually lost in the retraced line, the author considers it a very essential part of the letter.

Definiteness is essential in business writing. There should be a definite starting-point and a definite ending-point in every letter. Every curve and every loop should be definite and have a definite place in the plan of construction. In studying the forms of the letters here given, bear this in mind. Capital B may end in a dot as shown above, or it may end in an angular form, furnishing a connective stroke for the letters following.

The count for capital B is 1, 2, 3, and a fair practice speed is forty to the minute when the letters are disconnected, and a little higher rate when the letters are connected as in drill eighty-seven.

Drill 87

LESSON 72

Drill 88

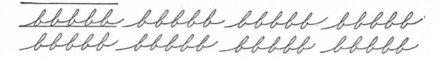

Study small b. The lower part of the letter should be as wide as the loop through the widest part, and some good penmen make it a little wider than this. Do not make your letters larger than those in the copy. Make line after line until you are able to make the letters easily and at a fair rate of speed. Sixteen groups or eighty letters to the minute is not a high rate for this drill. The count for each group is 1-2, 3-4, 5-6, 7-8, 9-10, with the emphasis on the finishing point in each letter. The connective stroke is slightly curved.

LESSON 73

Drill 89

Students are expected to practice the above words as movement drills. The speed in the first two lines should be from twenty to twenty-five words a minute. At this rate, form can be improved while movement is being developed. The word "billing" may be practiced at from twelve to fourteen a minute.

LESSON 74

Drill 90

hhhhh hhhhh hhhhh hhhhh
hhhhh hhhhh hhhhh hhhhh

Study the form before attempting the drill. Make ten sets of five each, or fifty small k's to the minute. Keep the letters down to the size of the copies. Count 1, 2, 3, for each letter with a slight check on the 2.

LESSON 75

Drill 91

This writing is large enough. In studying size, students should make frequent comparisons. The practice speed should be, for the first word, twenty, and for the word "killing" twelve to the minute. See the following page.

kill kill kill kill kill kill kill
kill kill kill kill kill kill kill
kill killing killing killing killing
kill killing killing killing killing

LESSON 76

TO RELIEVE MUSCULAR TENSION

It is often advantageous to go over the path of the letter, or exercise, with a dry pen. This method is especially helpful to a student whose muscles are hard, and who finds difficulty in overcoming the tendency to keep the muscles of the arm and body in a rigid condition. This plan has been suggested in former lessons, and we consider it of sufficient importance to receive emphasis here.

Another plan which the author has found helpful to students who write with strained muscles, is to place a weight on the paper, and write with the left arm hanging down. The tension of the right arm is relieved at once.

Still another plan to relieve this tension, so common among beginners, is to select some easy drill like o or m, and make it across the ruled lines with the eyes fixed upon some object at a distance on a level with them when the body is fairly erect.

Drill 92

Small f is a little shorter below than above the base line, and is closed on the base line. A fair rate of practice speed is fourteen groups of five letters each, or seventy letters to the minute. Count 1-2, 3-4, 5-6, 7-8, 9-10, for each group.

LESSON 77—Drill 93

full full full full full full full
fill fill fill fill fill fill fill

Write several lines of the first word before changing to the second. Write twenty or more words in a minute.

LESSON 78—Drill 94

fulfill fulfill fulfill fulfill fulfill
fulfill fulfill fulfill fulfill fulfill

Rate of practice speed, fourteen words to the minute. Good movement leads to good writing; good position leads to good movement. Watch the position; watch the movement.

LESSON 79

Let us emphasize the statement made in a preceding lesson that constant repetition is necessary in developing a good style of writing for business. Another thing for the student to bear in mind is the fact that the only way to learn to execute business writing is to practice business writing. Review as many lessons as time permits.

LESSON 80

Drill 95

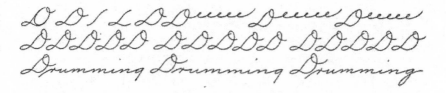

Compare the oval of capital D with capital O. Do not neglect to make a careful study of D, each part by itself, and the letter as a whole. Do not drag the hand over the paper, but keep it well up in front of the eyes, and drive it along firmly but lightly. It takes a little time, energy, and enthusiastic practice to make a good business penman, but it is encouraging to know that under the muscular movement plan there are no failures when favorable conditions prevail. Practice capital D until you can make forty-five fairly good letters to the minute. Count 1, 2, 3, for each letter.

In writing the word "Drumming" do not lift the pen from the beginning stroke in small r to the ending stroke of small g. Regularity and continuity of motion are very essential. Keep the pen on the paper. The word should be practiced at a rate of nine to a minute.

LESSON 81

Drill 96

Do not make the beginning part of capital T too high; it should be but little more than two-thirds the entire height of the letter. Note particularly that the last part curves over the top of the main (first) part without touching it. Time and hard work will be important factors in developing this letter. Be earnest, be faithful. The count is 1, 2, 3, 4, and about forty letters should be made to the minute.

Drill 97

You will see that this capital F is a copy of capital T, with the crossing added. This is not recommended as a business form, since it cannot be made rapidly. Many of the forms in this book are not given for their beauty, but because ninety per cent. of our best business penmen use them.

LESSON 82

Drill 98

In twelve of the business capitals we have the small loop beginning. Turn it up-side-down and you will see that it is the inverted figure six. Most pupils find this style of starting capital letters somewhat difficult at first, but when mastered it becomes a favorite. It is of sufficient importance to be given considerable study and practice.

A careful study and comparison of these capitals will show that in F, Q, W, X and Z the main downward strokes are curved much more than in H, K, M and N, while compound curves are used in the main strokes of U, V and Y.

Practice the first part at the left of the line.

LESSON 83

Drill 99

Capital Q, as shown above, is the enlarged form of figure two preceded by a movement drill. Curve the main downward strokes liberally. Make the lower loop flat on the base line and drop the finishing curve below. Students should frequently compare their writing with the copies.

Drill 100

The mind directs, the arm and hand perform; both mind and muscle must work in harmony.

No matter how perfectly the muscles of the arm are trained, good letters cannot be made unless a good conception of form *is in the mind*. Capital Q should be made well at the rate of sixty to the minute, and the figure two faster. The count in each case is 1, 2, 3.

Drill 101

ggggg ggggg ggggg ggggg

In the style of writing here presented the loop of small g extends three spaces below the base line. The paper should be held in such a position that the downward strokes are pulled toward the center of the body, the paper being changed from time to time with the left hand to keep its position relatively the same. The motion should be purely muscular throughtout, and the movement in making the loop particularly quick and elastic. Study the form closely and note the crossing of the loop with a left curve on the base. Pull the loops toward the center of the body and not toward the left elbow.

In groups of five connected letters a speed of sixty-five letters to the minute should be attained. A count of ten for each group of five will aid in regulating the movement.

Drill 102

By comparison it will be seen that q is a little shorter below the base than g; that the turn at the bottom is made to the right, instead of to the left; and that the lower part connects on the base line with the first. On account of the check at the connective point, fewer letters are made to the minute than of small g, but the movement should be quick.

LESSON 84

Drill 103

See suggestions at the top of the following page.

The inverted small e preceding capital H in page sixty-nine will not only aid in developing the small loop beginning but will insure freedom of movement and lightness of stroke.

Count 1, 2, 3, 4, for the drill and first part of capital H, and 1, 2, for the last part. In making the last part, swing the hand to the same direction as for the beginning of capital

O, but straighten the stroke from its center to its base. Let nothing escape you; observe closely every stroke, no matter how minute or unimportant it may appear.

Drill 104

With an easy, swinging movement, make thirty-five or more capitals of the above form to the minute with a count of 1, 2, 3, 4. The beginning loop may be made smaller than in the copy, but no larger in business writing.

Capital K is a natural companion to capital H. The beginning strokes in both letters are identical in size and shape.

LESSON 85

Drill 105

Careful study of the last part of K will be very much to the advantage of every student. Study it with the first part covered with a piece of paper. Turn the copy upside down and study it in that position. Notice particularly that the loop grasps the first part a little above the center.

Drill 106

KKKK KKKKK KKKK

Thirty-five to forty to the minute will be a fair rate of speed. Compare your capitals frequently with the copy.

Are you studying the instructions? They tell you just how to succeed.

LESSON 86—Drill 107

Humming Humming Humming H

This is a most excellent word to practice at this stage of the work. It is a good movement-developer. Give close attention to size, general appearance, and space between letters, and guard against irregular movement. Keep the hand well up in front of the eyes and drive the pen lightly. Write a half page of the copy and then make a careful study of your work. Try to write each line better than the preceding. Three words should be written to the line.

LESSON 87—Drill 108

A REVIEW

Work faithfully on every letter. Repeat the forms over and over until decided improvement can be seen. Make frequent comparisons. Study length, breadth, curves, and connections closely.

Rate of speed to the minute: F, fifty; H; thirty-five; K, thirty-five; M, thirty-five; N, forty.

LESSON 88

Drill 109

A REVIEW

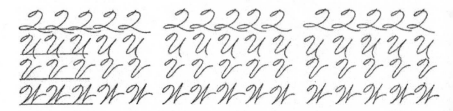

Rate of practice speed: Q, sixty; U, forty-five; V, fifty-five; W, forty to the minute.

Points to Observe—Capital Q is the enlarged form of figure two. The last parts of U, V, and W are shorter than the other parts, and the first strokes in U and V are exactly alike. In capital W, check the motion a little at the base line in the first main downward stroke, as this will aid in the construction of the last part.

LESSON 89

Drill 110

Practice this compact oval as a beginning drill. Make it, between two ruled lines, carry the pen lightly and see how many you can make in one row, with one dip of ink.

Study and compare as you practice. Drill speed to the minute in the following capitals: X, thirty-five; Y, forty; Z, fifty.

Drill 111

REVIEW WORK

At this point it would be a good plan to review all the essential work of the preceding lessons. From one to two weeks should be spent in such practice.

LESSON 90

Drill 112

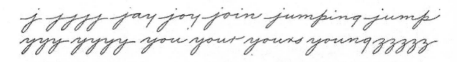

Some authors make the loop of j and z shorter below the base than small y and g, but we make no distinction. The j begins like a small i and ends with a loop. Small z should receive careful attention.

LESSON 91

SOMETHING MORE ABOUT SIZE

In these lessons is presented a style of writing that is easily and rapidly executed, and though large enough to be perfectly legible it is small enough for general use. Examine the writing of the best business penmen in the large mercantile centers and it will be seen that this is true.

It is a grave error to present for practice models larger than the pupils are expected to employ in their ordinary writing. And yet many professional penmen continue to present models not only two or three times larger than good business writing is expected to be, but forms that cannot possibly be executed at commercial speed.

CAPITAL AND WORD PRACTICE AS MOVEMENT DRILLS

In the following copies the capital and word practice is intended to encourage free movement, continuity in execution, and better control of the writing muscles than has, perhaps, been gained. The plan is to repeat the capital until it can be made at the speed designated, and to follow with word practice. In the word drills the value of a continuous movement must not be lost sight of, and the pen should remain on the paper from the beginning to the ending of the small letters. In fact, all the copies should be treated as movement drills. Words ending in "ing" have been purposely selected and their value will not be questioned if they are rightly practiced.

Drill 113

The rate of speed for capital A is from seventy-five to eighty-five to the minute and for the word "Alling", about fifteen to the minute.

LESSON 92—Drill 114

CCCCC CCCCC CCCCC
Calling Calling Calling Calling
Chiming Chiming Chiming Chiming

Practice the word "Calling" at fifteen or more a minute, and "Chiming" at the same rate.

LESSON 93

Drill 115

OOOOO OOOOO OOOOO
Oiling Oiling Oiling Oiling Oiling

LESSON 94

Drill 116

LLLLL LLLLL LLLLL
Lanning Lanning Lanning Lanning

Open the lesson with a drill on capital O, making fully sixty to the minute, and write the word "Oiling" at the rate of fourteen to the minute. Watch position; watch movement.

Capital L, rightly practiced, is always an excellent movement drill.

Questions you should be able to answer intelligently: Where and how does the beginning stroke start? How long is the upper loop, compared with the length of the letter? Is the downward stroke a straight line or a curve? Is the lower loop round or flat, and what part rests on the base line? Is the final stroke finished on or below the base line?

Compare your work with the copy in reference to these questions. Practice speed, sixty letters to the minute. Write the word "Lanning" with a very light motion at ass-peed not less than twelve to the minute.

LESSON 95—Drill 117

Do not overlook the proportions of capital M. It should fill a square. Practice speed for M, about forty to the minute, and of the word "Milling", fourteen words a minute; a higher rate of speed may be applied by some pupils.

LESSON 96

Special Notice—Pupils who cannot use and apply the muscular movement fairly well, should return to the beginning lessons and review them, studying carefully all the instructions regarding position, penholding, and methods of developing movement.

Drill 118

N N N N N   N N N N N   N N N N N
Nulling Nulling Nulling Nulling

Capital N should be made at the rate of fifty-five a minute. Practice speed for "Nulling", fourteen or sixteen to the minute.

LESSON 97—Drill 119

H H H H H   H H H H H   H H H H H
Hauling Hauling Hauling Hauling

Capital H should be made at the rate of thirty-five or forty a minute, and the word "Hauling" about fifteen to the minute.

LESSON 98

Drill 120

KKKKK KKKKK KKKKK
Killing Killing Killing Killing Kill

Forty capital K's to the minute is a fair rate. Pupils should not lose sight of the fact that motion determines form. Take care of the motion and the forms of the letters will develop easily and naturally. A careful study of the movement as applied to capital K will be helpful. After making the first part of the letter, the hand (with the pen in the air) should swing below the base line, describing an oval and returning upward to the beginning point of the last part of the letter. Be sure to connect the parts with a loop, as shown in the copy. Drop the finishing part below the base line. Don't forget the word practice; about twelve words to the minute is a fair rate of speed.

LESSON 99

Drill 121

PPPPP PPPPP PPPPP
Pulling Pulling Pulling Pulling

Practice capital P at the rate of fifty to sixty letters a minute;

the word "Pulling", twelve words a minute. Some pupils will be able to write the word at higher speed and still do good work.

LESSON 100

Be sure to fix in mind the image of the letter before attempting it. Study closely the proportions and the direction of every stroke. Make about fifty capital R's to the minute, as given in the next page.

Do not forget that your advancement depends upon movement, and that movement depends much upon position. The body should be self-supporting, with the feet resting squarely on the floor, and should not crowd against the desk; the right arm should be well out from the side; the right hand well in front of the eyes; and the paper twelve or fourteen inches from the eyes.

If the wrist or side of the hand rests on the paper, all motion coming from the muscles of the arm will stop at the wrist and it will be an impossibility to use muscular movement. Watch the wrist and the side of the hand closely. Remember that the propelling power is above the elbow, in the upper arm and shoulder.

Write line after line of the word "Running" with a light, quick motion, and compare with the copy frequently. Twelve to fourteen words should be written to the minute.

Drill 122

RRRRR RRRRR RRRRR
Running Running Running Run

LESSON 101

Drill 123

SSSSS SSSSS SSSSS
Swelling Swelling Swelling Swelling

Turn to lesson fifty-four and practice and study capital S in accordance with the instructions. Enough time should be reserved to write at least one page of the word "Swelling".

LESSON 102

Drill 124

Pupils who cannot make good loop letters should make a special study of lesson thirty-two.

GGGGG GGGGG GGGGG
Galling Galling Galling Galling

LESSON 103

Drill 125

2 2 2 2 2   2 2 2 2 2   2 2 2 2 2
Quelling Quelling Quelling Quell

As explained in a former lesson, capital Q is simply a large figure two. It is a good movement drill. Practice it as such. In all your word practice a special effort should be made to space the letters evenly. Study your written lines with that in mind.

LESSON 104

Pupils should give particular attention to the appearance of their finished pages, making letters and words conform to spaces. The capitals should occupy only from two-thirds to three-fourths the distance between the ruled lines, assuming that they are about three-eighths of an inch apart.

From fifteen to twenty capitals should be made to a line. If the forms are well made, a page of capitals written in accordance with these suggestions will present a very pleasing appearance. See drill 126.

The crossing of capital F at the top of the following page is above the center, and the final stroke at the crossing is small. In practice, write the full word every time the capital is made. Do not let your practice work approach scribbling. Do the very best you can, not part of the time, but all the time.

You aim before you sheet. You should study the instructions before you practice the drills.

Drill 126

Filling Filling Filling Filling Filling

LESSON 105—Drill 127

Inning Inning Inning Inning I

Always start capital I with an upward stroke from below the base line. The upper part should be about one-half the width of the lower. The crossing of the beginning with the main downward stroke should be one space above the base line. Practice the detached capital as well as the word until there is an improvement in the movement and its application.

LESSON 106—Drill 128

Judging Judging Judging Judging

Practice and compare, and then practice again. Capital J is

127

twice as wide above as below the base, and the lower part is a little shorter than the upper part. Pupils who find the letter troublesome should review lessons forty-nine and fifty.

LESSON 107—Drill 129

E E E E E E E E E E E E E E E
Elling Ending Elling Ending Elling

Write a page of capital E's and another page of the words.

LESSON 108—Drill 130

B B B B B B B B B B B B B B B
Billing Billing Billing Billing

Capital B was discussed at considerable length in lesson seventy-one, and students who have failed to master the letter should turn to that lesson for review.

LESSON 109—Drill 131

D D D D D D D D D D D D D D D
Drilling Drilling Drilling Drilling

Make your letters no larger than the copies. Write line after line of the detached capitals before writing the word. Rate of speed for practice, fifty to fifty-five capitals and fourteen words in a minute.

LESSON 110—Drill 132

Twilling Twilling Twilling Twilling

The first part of capital T should be no more than two-thirds the height of the entire letter. Give attention to the abrupt stop on the base line in the first part of the letter. Carry the last part up and over the first part in a graceful curve. Practice the word as well as the detached capital.

LESSON 111—Drill 133

Willing Willing Willing Willing Will

Capital W should be very closely studied. The tendency is to slant the last part too much, tipping it away from the first part. The upward stroke beginning the second part is a right curve, and the construction of the last part and the appearance of the entire letter are to a considerable extent dependent upon that line.

In making the first part there should be a stop at the base

line. This will aid very much in the construction of the last part of the letter. The last line in the letter, it will be noticed, is shorter than the two center strokes. It is unlikely that students who fail to study its construction closely will learn to make a good capital W. The rate should be between forty and fifty letters to a minute. Do not neglect the word practice.

Write about sixteen words to the minute.

LESSON 112—Drill 134

The last part of capital U is shorter than the first part. Study the letter until you have a good mental picture of it. Make U at the rate of forty-five to a minute, and do not neglect the word practice.

LESSON 113

Drill 135

An otherwise good capital V will be spoiled if the finishing line is too long. Notice its length. Study and practice should go hand in hand. Do not neglect either.

CAUTION TO TEACHERS AND PUPILS

The development of good business writing is dependent, first, upon proper clothing of the writing arm; second, upon a substantial desk or table of the right height; third, upon a good position at the desk; fourth, upon a relaxed condition of the writing muscles; fifth, upon the freedom of the wrist and the side of the hand from the paper; and sixth, upon concentration, determination, and constantly repeated effort.

Teachers who cannot maintain enthusiasm throughout the writing period, and who do not realize the necessity of constantly repeated cautions and admonitions, must never expect to secure flattering results.

Teachers, see that your pupils are alert, watchful, and practicing under the most favorable conditions. Force upon the inner consciousness of every pupil the harmfulness of careless practice and the necessity for making every stroke according to instructions and in the right direction.

Pupils, do not vehemently assert that you are very anxious to become good penmen, and then abuse the opportunities within your reach. Learning to write well is not difficult to the earnest, careful, hard-working pupil; and with such, results ahnoot immediately follow correct methods of practice.

Finger movement and muscular movement are antagonistic, and the student who makes an effort to use muscular movement in the writing class only, need not hope for success.

Home students, not having the advantage of the directing counsel of good teachers, should frequently review the beginning lessons. You cannot fail if you follow the instructions.

Drill 136

I am pining for a pin to use in pinning
I am pining for a pin to use in pinning

Practice the above copy in sections. Repeat capital I until the form is good when made rapidly, follow with several lines of the word "am," and continue to practice each word in the copy until uniformity in spacing, height, and slant have been developed. Then write a page of the complete copy and criticise it.

As simple as it looks, there is material for several hours' practice in this copy.

LESSON 114—Drill 137

A B Collins owns the mill on the hill
A B Collins owns the mill on the hill

The same method of practice should be followed in this drill as in the preceding one.

LESSON 115—Drill 138

Begin this lesson with your usual movement drills.

Specimens of my business penmanship
Specimens of my business penmanship

First practice drill one hundred and thirty-eight in sections, word by word. Follow with a full page of the completed copy, and do not neglect to criticise results. Height, spacing, and slant should receive special attention.

REGULAR

In the following lessons are given copies in line-writing from which pages should be written. It may be easy for some students who cannot maintain uniform excellence throughout a page to write one or two lines well. The object of your practice should be attractive work and commercial speed. To attain this end, study the appearance of the finished line and page from time to time, and always try to harmonize the writing with the space it occupies.

LESSON 116—Drill 139

Always study drill before practicing.

Practice this copy as given. Write each word over and over,

until the motion used is almost automatic and a marked improvement is shown in the general appearance. Then write a few lines of the drill complete, and study the appearance.

LESSON 117—Drill 140

Be sure to use a good rapid movement.

Do not rest a moment until you have filled one page with this copy; then judge the appearance as a whole. Do not write larger than the copy.

LESSON 118—Drill 141

Do not fail to see and correct all errors.

Make a few lines of capital D before writing the line.

Do not lose sight of the fact that position at the desk has much to do with the development of writing. Position refers to feet, body, arms, wrist, fingers, pen, head, and paper. In preceding lessons enough has been said about these to make extended instructions here unnecessary.

LESSON 119—Drill 142

Faithfully fulfill all promises. Final

Uniformity may be hard to maintain in this copy. After writing a few lines pick out the faults and endeavor to correct them.

LESSON 120—Drill 143

Good business writing is in demand.

Solid pages are wanted; not haphazard writing.

LESSON 121—Drill 144

Hold happiness more sacred than gold.

Practice capital H as a movement drill a few minutes before writing the complete line Maintain equal distances, not only between letters, but between the words.

LESSON 122—Drill 145

Join letters with care and judgment.

LESSON 123—Drill 146

Keep thinking Keep moving Keep gliding.

LESSON 124—Drill 147

Louis Lanning paid his account in full.

LESSON 125—Drill 148

Mills and Milligan are good millers.

Drill 149

Nine months after date I promise to pay.

LESSON 126—Drill 150

One by one the sands are flowing One.

Practice capital O as a movement drill for a few minutes and
then do your best on the entire copy.

LESSON 127—Drill 151

Pull push and practice penmanship.

136

LESSON 128—Drill 152

Quibbling and quarreling are bad habits.

This drill is difficult enough to merit careful practice for a full writing period. It will be best first to practice capital Q as a movement drill.

LESSON 129—Drill 153

Rolling muscular movement is the best.

LESSON 130—Drill 154

Summer sunshine follows spring.

LESSON 131—Drill 155

Time and tide wait for no man.

LESSON 132—Drill 156

Important improvement in penmanship.

LESSON 133—Drill 157

Union of interests brings union of minds.

It is always a good plan, where time permits, to practice each capital at the beginning of the line as a drill.

LESSON 134—Drill 158

Value your time as you value money.

Do not neglect the movement drills, although they are not specially mentioned in every lesson.

LESSON 135—Drill 159

Willing William was willing to watch.

LESSON 136—Drill 160

Xenophon fixed historical events.

Capital X is made with a figure six inverted, and a figure six right side up. Keep this in mind when making it.

LESSON 137—Drill 161

Young man grasp your opportunity.

LESSON 138—Drill 162

Zero weather gives zest to pedestrians.

LESSON 139—Drill 163

Pay James C Robinson on demand $4175623.

LESSON 140—Drill 164

Due E. F. Gilman Nine Hundred Dimes.
Due E. F. Gilman Nine Hundred Dimes.

Work up to the complete copy by a systematic practice on
the capitals and words separately.

LESSON 141—Drill 165

CPR CPR CPR CPR CPR CPR

The author, in common with many teachers of business

writing, has found the practice of combinations of capitals very helpful in developing accuracy and freedom. This is an excellent part of the course in which to introduce such drills, but tangled and difficult combinations should be avoided.

Drill one hundred and sixty-five, if rightly practiced, will insure light movement and develop constructive ability. About twenty-two of this combination should be made to a minute. It will be profitable to devote a full session to it.

LESSON 142

Drills 166 and 167

Practice the combinations of capitals several minutes before practicing the small letters. A perfect mastery of the following combinations will help students in the work that follows. A few scattered lines will not meet the requirements. Write a full page.

LESSON 143—Drill 168

Use uniform motion from beginning to end, and make about twenty-five to a minute.

A.N.Palmer A.N.Palmer A.N.Palmer

LESSON 144—Drill 169

H H H H H H H   H H H H H H H

This affords a good drill and a good test of accuracy in applying movement. The last downward stroke in capital H is a left curve, is it not? Study the direction of the pen in making it, and then strike boldly. This will be a good drill to practice frequently at the beginning of a lesson.

Drill 170

P.H.Keller   P.H.Keller   P.H.Keller

Use your eyes, focus your mind upon your work, study and practice earnestly, and you will be pleased with the results.

LESSON 145

Movement drills for a few minutes and then the following:

Drill 171

O.P.Daniels   O.P.Daniels   O.P.Daniels

Practice the combination of capitals several times before making the small letters. Such repeated effort will be helpful.

LESSON 146

Drill 172

E.G. Palmer C.B. Palmer J.B. Palmer

This is a specimen of the Palmer Method penmanship. It combines legibility, rapidity, ease and endurance.

It is not so much the amount of practice, as the kind of practice that counts. It is the constant effort to acquire precision that leads to success in writing.

It is not so much the amount of practice, as the kind of practice that counts. It is the constant effort to acquire precision that leads to success in writing.

It is not so much the amount of practice, as the kind of practice that counts. It is the constant effort to acquire precision that leads to success in writing.

YourTown, Jan. 30, 1915.

The A.N. Palmer Co.,
New York City.

Gentlemen;- I have completed the lessons in the Palmer Method of Business Writing, and herewith submit my examination. I have tried to follow closely the printed instructions in the manual, and hope to obtain a Final Certificate.

Awaiting your decision, I am,
Sincerely,

	Count	Number per Minute		Count	Number per Minute		Count	Number per Minute		Count	Number per Minute		Count	Number per Minute
A	1-2	75	K	1-2-3-4	33 to 40	U	1-2-3	45	e	1	28 groups of 5 or 140	p	1-2	12 groups of 5 or 60
B	1-2-3	40	L	1-2	50 to 55	V	1-2	55	f	1-2	14 groups of 5 or 70	q	1-2	10 groups of 5 or 50
C	1-2	70	M	1-2-3-4	30 to 33	W	1-2-3-4	40	g	1-2	13 groups of 5 or 65	r	1-2	18 groups of 5 or 90
D	1-2-3	45	N	1-2-3	40	X	1-2-3	35	h	1-2	14 groups of 5 or 70	s	1-2	17 groups of 5 or 85
E	1-2-3	45 to 50	O	1-2	70	Y	1-2-3-4	40	i	1	10 groups of 5 or 50	t	1	20 groups of 5 or 100
F	1-2-3	50	P	1-2	50 to 60	Z	1-2-3	30	j	1-2	14 groups of 5 or 70	u	1-2	12 groups of 4 or 48
G	1-2-3	40 to 50	Q	1-2-3	60	a	1-2	14 groups of 5 or 70	k	1-2-3	10 groups of 5 or 50	v	1-2	12 groups of 5 or 60
H	1-2-3-4	33	R	1-2-3	45	b	1-2	16 groups of 5 or 80	l	1	25 groups of 5 or 125	w	1-2-3	12 groups of 5 or 60
I	1-2-3	45	S	1-2	45 to 50	c	1-2	16 groups of 5 or 80	m	1-2-3	12 groups of 4 or 48	x	1	18 groups of 5 or 90
J	1-3	60 to 70	T	1-2-3-4	40	d	1-2	13 groups of 5 or 65	n	1-2	18 groups of 5 or 90	y	1-2	14 groups of 5 or 70
									o	1-2	18 groups of 5 or 90	z	1-2	14 groups of 5 or 70

PUPIL'S CERTIFICATE, KNOWN AS THE DIPLOMA

THIS HAS BEEN GREATLY REDUCED. ORIGINAL SIZE, 14x17 INCHES

Made in the USA
San Bernardino, CA
08 April 2016